#startupeverywhere

Startup Guide Nagoya

EDITORIAL
Publisher: Sissel Hansen
Editor: Hazel Boydell
Proofreaders: Ted Hermann, Michelle Mills Smith

PRODUCTION
Global Production Lead: Eglė Duleckytė
Community Managers: Daphne Frühmann,
Jiske van Straaten
Local Production Managers: Tatsuya Hirose,
Tomozo Yagi, Shoko Matsumoto
Local Production Support: Paul Lee Wang
Research by Chiara Lo Zito, Sofia Chatrian

DESIGN & PHOTOGRAPHY
Designer: Cat Serafim
Illustrations by Cat Serafim , Daniela Castanheira,
Joana Carvalho
Photo Editors: Cat Serafim, Joana Carvalho
Photography Coordinator: Tessy Morelli

PARTNERSHIPS
COO: Anna Weissensteiner
anna@startupguide.com

Printed by
Medialis-Offsetdruck GmbH
Heidelbergerstraße 65, 12435 Berlin

Published by Startup Guide World ApS
Borgbjergsvej 1, 2450 Copenhagen

info@startupguide.com
startupguide.com

Worldwide distribution by Die Gestalten
gestalten.com

ISBN: 978-989-54894-1-1

WRITERS
Anthony Griffin (IBIDEN P. 94, NTT West P. 100, Toyota Industries P. 112)
Carter Witt (Startups P. 34-55, Programs P. 58-65, Spaces P. 68-91,
Founders P. 120-159, Schools P. 162-173, Investors P. 176-189)
L. Isaac Simon (PwC Japan Group P. 106)
Phoebe Amoroso (Essentials P. 16, Overview P. 18-31)

LOCAL RESEARCH AND DATA
Carter Witt (Directory P. 190-194)
Naoki Inagaki (Overview P.18-19, Directory P. 190-194)
Noriko Kato (Directory P. 190-194)
Noritaka Yamashita (Directory P. 190-194)
Yuki Goto (Overview P.18-19, Directory P. 190-194)

PHOTOGRAPHER
Photography by Noir (noir-e.com)

ADDITIONAL PHOTOGRAPHY
Peter Bjerke P. 8 / Nagoya City P. 6-7, 18 /
Nagoya Cityscape Design Selection/Horikawa Flower
Festival Executive Committee P. 21 / Nagoya Castle General
Administration Office P. 26 / Nagoya Cityscape Design Selection P. 28 /
Kazuki Takano P. 34 / Shunsuke Shishiba P. 60 /
Tomohiro Ueta P. 64 / TVC Co,. Ltd P. 77-79 /
Kouki Hatano P. 81-83 / WeWORK P. 89-91 /
Said Karlsson P. 106, 108-109 / GLOBIS University P. 164 /
Nagoya Institute of Technology official photographer P. 168 /
Shunichi Oda P. 176 / Hoejin Iwai P. 30 and Jet Dela Cruz P. 195
from Unsplash.com

onetreeplanted.org

STARTUP GUIDE NAGOYA

STARTUP GUIDE NAGOYA

In partnership with
Nagoya Innovator's Garage

Proudly supported by

INNOVATOR'S
GARAGE

Sissel Hansen
/ Startup Guide

Nagoya is the heart of Japan's manufacturing industry and a city that demonstrates true innovation. You'll find cutting-edge technology and modern production methods here, as well as first-class research institutions and a quickly growing community of startups and support programs.

With shifting attitudes toward entrepreneurship and the country's strong legacy in tech innovation, Japan's startup scene is increasingly drawing attention from international entrepreneurs and investors, and Nagoya is one of the most appealing hubs. Dedicated government efforts to encourage entrepreneurship and support centers such as Japan External Trade Organization (JETRO) Invest Japan Business Support Center (IBSC) Nagoya make it easier for foreigners to navigate the local business community than ever before. Nagoya's central location, affordability and excellent rail links to other parts of the country also make it a great place to be based.

Nagoya Innovator's Garage is a key part of the local startup community. It fosters collaboration among founders, government, academia and others, and promotes open exchange of ideas through its events and programs. For newcomers to the city, it's an invaluable source of contacts and support.

Technology is a huge part of the local ecosystem, with a number of programs dedicated to teaching both ICT and business skills to aspiring entrepreneurs, such as Nagoya ICT Innovation Lab and the AI/IoT-focused Nagoya BOOST 10000 program. i Smart Technologies uses IoT technology to improve factory productivity, and Optimind has created proprietary algorithms that help it optimize delivery routes. Biotech is also strongly represented in Nagoya – Craif's nanowire device allows early cancer detection and United Immunity combines nanotechnology and immunotherapy to treat disease.

We hope you find this book both inspiring and informative, and that it helps you successfully navigate Nagoya's startup ecosystem.

Sissel Hansen
Founder and CEO of Startup Guide

Takashi Kawamura
/ Mayor of Nagoya City

Nagoya has always been home to people with a pioneering spirit. The citizens of this region have consistently created new businesses. From timber and textiles to aviation and automobiles, Nagoya is a world-class manufacturing center. It is a city where new industries are born and grow. Today, this pioneering spirit is evident in deeptech startups that are joining forces with manufacturers and first-class research institutes and universities to solve social issues.

Aichi Prefecture had the third-largest amount of funds raised by startup companies in Japan in 2019. The abundance of ideas, technologies and support services necessary for startups to grow is now giving new companies a tailwind. The many large companies based in Nagoya are instrumental in supporting the startup ecosystem, and smart human resources are further driving the local economy and actively engaging in innovation activities. Nagoya Innovator's Garage was launched to make connections among these local companies, startups and individuals and foster collaboration.

In 2020, Aichi-Nagoya was named as a "startup ecosystem global hub city" by the Cabinet Office. This ecosystem aims to realize growth that drives the Japan economy, and the creation of startups and new industries continues to promote innovation in this central Japan region. We are firmly working together with industries and universities to form a globally cohesive innovation and startup ecosystem by utilizing the deeptech and manufacturing knowledge that are the strengths of this region.

To realize our vision, we encourage more startups and entrepreneurs to come to Nagoya, where they will be very welcome.

Takashi Kawamura
Mayor of Nagoya City

Local Community Partner
/ Nagoya Innovator's Garage

Nagoya is the fourth-biggest city in Japan and the economic, industrial and administrative core of the central Japan region. The manufacturing industry is a prominent feature of this area, with activities related to six resources: water, soil, wood, yarn, iron and Nagoya's well-established road links to other cities. Traditional crafts were born from these rich resources, with people in the region paving the way in superior quality goods for more than four hundred years. Today, almost a fourth of Japan's market share of shipments of manufactured goods comes from the Nagoya area.

Nagoya's startup ecosystem and sustainable manufacturing industry have been gradually generated and are still growing. Our role is to connect the various players and strengthen their collaborations. Recently, our consortium has been certified by the Cabinet Office as a global startup city, accelerating the building of a manufacturing-based startup ecosystem in the central region of Japan.

With easy access to Tokyo, Kyoto and Osaka and situated close to the Central Japan International Airport, Nagoya is a convenient location for business. It is also a gateway for journeys north into Japan's impressive mountains and a great base for day trips elsewhere. Reasonable living costs and office fees and links to major universities are other assets to being based in Nagoya.

Nagoya Innovator's Garage is excited to be a part of *Startup Guide Nagoya* and to help highlight the many impressive entrepreneurs, accelerators and investors featured in the book. If you're even a little curious about Nagoya, this is a great place to start. We welcome you to be a part of the startup ecosystem here and are open to meeting new entrepreneurs from all over the world. There is much business potential still buried in Nagoya, and we welcome you to explore it with us.

Hirooki Fujiwara
Director General, Nagoya Innovator's Garage

Noritaka Yamashita
General Manager, Nagoya Innovator's Garage

contents

STARTUP
GUIDE
NAGOYA

Local Ecosystem

[Facts & Figures]
- Nagoya is one of the most concentrated manufacturing areas in the world, with a GDP of ¥82 trillion across the wider central Japan region.
- Manufacturing accounts for 36% of GDP by industry.
- The majority of new ventures are born from research at local institutes including Nagoya University and Nagoya Institute of Technology.
- The number of ventures coming out of Nagoya University more than doubled between 2015 and 2017, and the growth rate is among the highest in Japan.
- The amount of funds raised by startup companies in Aichi Prefecture, where Nagoya is located, was the third-largest amount raised in Japan by prefecture in 2019.
- R&D spending in the central Japan region amounts to ¥2.4 trillion yen, meaning there is plenty of scope for startup investment.
- Nagoya uses the Japanese yen (¥). The average exchange rate over the twelve months before publication was ¥1 = $0.009315.

[Notable Startups]
- Tier IV created the world's first foundation that facilitates development and production of open-source software for autonomous driving. Its total funding to date is $166 million.
- Prodrone manufactures drones for professional use. In 2016, it launched the world's first dual robot arm large-format drone.
- In collaboration with Nagoya University, Craif is combining its original device with machine learning to develop a highly accurate, non-invasive, cancer-diagnosis system.

Sources: Nagoya City, "Tier IV Raises Total Funding to $166 Million for Open Source Autonomous Driving Systems" (tier4.jp), "Developed the world's first large direct work type drone 'PD6B-AW-ARM' with two robot arms" (prodrone.com), craif.com

[City] # Nagoya, Japan

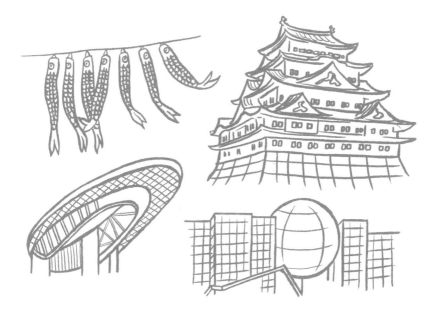

[Statistics]   Urban population: 2.3 million
Area: 326.5 km^2
Population density: 7,121 per km^2
GDP: $128 billion

Nagoya Castle – Nagoya, Japan

Intro to the City

Nagoya is the fourth-largest city in Japan by population, and the central Japan region is home to around 17 million people, making it a thriving place to both work and live. It's a true industrial powerhouse: from automobiles to aerospace, it boasts the country's largest concentration of high-tech industries, with many companies ranking among the top in their field.

Toyota Motor, Mitsubishi Heavy Industries and machine-tools manufacturer Mori Seiki are just some of the big players, and the region also has a wide base of SMEs with excellent technological capabilities. The Nagoya area accounts for around one-fifth of the shipping value of all Japan's manufactured goods. This expertise is supported by many local universities and research institutes, which provide a supply of skilled personnel. In July 2020, Aichi-Nagoya was identified by the Cabinet Office as a "startup ecosystem global hub city." The goal is to develop the area into a deeptech hub by combining its research strengths and manufacturing experience, spurring startup creation in a broad range of industries including mobility, aviation, healthcare, food, agriculture and infrastructure.

Life in Nagoya is comfortable – it has all the benefits of a big city with a more laid-back vibe, fewer crowds and shorter commuting times. In a public-opinion survey in 2019, over 90 percent of residents described it as an easy place to live.. Access to other cities is excellent, with Osaka and Tokyo easily reached by train. Locals love to dine out, from enjoying morning coffee to visiting lively *izakaya* (Japanese-style pubs) at night. There is a good reason *Nagoya meshi* (Nagoya cuisine) has fans nationwide.

Before You Come

Nagoya's winters are cool and crisp with minimal precipitation but summers are hot and humid, so make sure to bring a range of clothing. Budget both time and money to stay in a hotel or short-term rental while you search for accommodation – finding an apartment may require some perseverance. You will need a valid work or long-term-stay visa (not a ninety-day tourist visa) in order to sign a tenancy agreement and open a bank account, so be sure to check what documents you need to bring for your visa application. Unfortunately, the visa process can be cumbersome and will require at least two visits to the Immigration Bureau (**immi-moj.go.jp**). Nagoya has a good subway and bus network, but the suburbs are most easily accessed by car. If you have a driver's license, check whether your country of residence is valid to convert directly to a Japanese one and whether you fulfill the conditions. If not, you will need to take a written and practical test in Japan.

Visas and Work Permits

If you're entering Japan on a job contract, your employer will sponsor you and apply for the appropriate category of visa. There are multiple categories, including professor, artist and highly skilled professional. One of the most common is the Engineer/Specialist in Humanities/International Services Visa, which is a broad category that includes professions ranging from software engineers to designers. All work visas require you to obtain a Certificate of Eligibility, which you can apply for in person or by proxy at the Immigration Bureau in Japan or at your regional Japanese Embassy. Typically, the company making the job offer will do this for you.

If you're looking to start your own business, you must establish your right to reside in Japan, which involves fairly strict conditions. Fortunately, Aichi Prefecture has been designated a National Strategic Special Zone and is part of a program to support foreign entrepreneurship in the region. This allows prospective foreign entrepreneurs to obtain a visa while preparing to meet the requirements. You must submit a business plan and obtain a certificate that confirms the business startup activity. This takes about two weeks. If successful, you will be able to apply to the Immigration Bureau and receive a business management visa. This gives you six months to complete the necessary preparations and take the appropriate steps to incorporate. For more information, visit **pref.aichi.jp/soshiki/kinyu/gaikokujinsogyo.html.** Aichi-Nagoya International Business Access Center (I-BAC) (**i-bac.jp**) and Station Ai (**aichi-startup.jp/english**) can also provide consultation in English.

See **Important Government Offices** page **193**

Horikawa – Nagoya, Japan

Osu Kannon – Nagoya, Japan

Cultural Differences

Nagoya boasts a colorful culture, and locals love traditional celebrations. Annual events include the Nagoya Festival and the Port Festival, which features fireworks and a water-logging contest. Nagoya's cuisine is renowned and varied – try miso sauces, peppered chicken wings and charcoal-grilled eel. There is also the custom of morning service: coffee shops offer a free simple breakfast alongside a cup of coffee. It can take some time to build business relationships in Japan, and direct confrontation is usually avoided. Socializing outside the office is often expected, with *nomikai* ("drinking meetings") helping to soften the rigidity of the boardroom and serving as an arena for new ideas. Nagoya's citizens have a reputation for their practical approach, and the region's products and services are known to be founded in common sense. It's often said that if you can succeed at business in Nagoya, you'll succeed in Japan.

Cost of Living

Despite being one of Japan's major cities, the cost of living in Nagoya is relatively low. The average monthly expenses per household of two or more members with at least one earner is ¥287,547 compared to ¥332,517 in Tokyo. Rent is less than 60 percent of the cost in the capital. The average monthly rent for a studio or one-bedroom apartment within ten minutes' walk from a subway or train station ranges from ¥43,500 in Moriyama Ward in the northeast to ¥63,600 in the more centrally located Higashi Ward. Japanese companies typically cover the cost of commuting for employees. Dining out is very affordable for Japan, with lunchtime meals from as little as ¥500. The average price of a 500 mL bottle of beer at a restaurant is ¥566, below the national average of ¥592. Nagoya City offers subsidies towards the cost of children's healthcare, including hospitalization and outpatients visits, as well as free healthcare checkups.

Accommodation

Sharing apartments is uncommon in Japan and so there are many compact apartments aimed at single people. Some options can be found online (check out **suumo.jp**) but people usually use estate agents in their area of choice. Visit a few to compare their listings and fees, and note that not all properties will accept foreign residents. Nagoya International Center (**nic-nagoya.or.jp**) has a Nagoya Living Guide document in several languages and can provide help. Expect to pay more than three months' rent up front: a deposit, a cleaning fee, agency fees and key money, which is a nonrefundable payment to the landlord. You will also need a guarantor in Japan willing to cover you should you default on your rent. Several companies provide this service for a one-off fee of roughly 50–100 percent of your monthly rent. Apartments are almost always unfurnished, so be prepared to buy everything – even light bulbs!

See **Accommodation** page **192**

Oasis21 – Nagoya, Japan

Insurance

Enrollment in *shakai hoken* (social insurance) is mandatory in Japan. If you are an employee, your employer will enroll you in the healthcare system known as *kenkō hoken*, which covers 70 percent of any medical claims. Your premium depends on your income, but your employer will pay half and deduct the other half from your monthly salary. They will also enroll you in the *kosei nenkin*, the pension system, and again, you and your employer each bear half of the cost. Other monthly deductions include *koyō hoken* (unemployment insurance) and *rōsai hoken* (worker's accident compensation). If you are a freelancer, you have to visit your local ward office to enroll yourself in the healthcare and pension systems. You will pay *kokumin kenkō hoken* (health insurance) based on your age and previous year's income, and *kokumin nenkin* (pension), which is ¥16,550 per month as of 2020.

See **Insurance Companies** page **193**

Starting a Company

To acquire the relevant visa to operate a company in Japan, prospective foreign entrepreneurs must open an office and either invest at least ¥5 million or employ at least two people. If you're bringing employees from overseas, you must sponsor their visas too. Given this, it is definitely worth taking advantage of the business-management visa program, which will give you extra time to prepare to meet these requirements. Foreigners who are about to graduate from a university in Japan and establish their business in Aichi Prefecture can apply for the special regional Aichi Startup Visa. Finding an office space can take time, but you may be eligible for temporary free office space provided by Japan External Trade Organization (JETRO). Contact Invest Japan Business Support (IBSC) Nagoya (jetro.go.jp/en/invest/ibsc) to find out more.

Once you've established your residence status, you can proceed with the incorporation process. In Japan, the majority of companies are registered as *kabushiki kaisha* (joint stock companies) or *gōdō kaisha* (limited liability corporations). Kabushiki kaisha are typically larger and command a certain amount of prestige when dealing with business partners and clients, but they also require more paperwork and initial investment. Gōdō kaisha are not required to submit Articles of Incorporation, establish a board of directors or hold member meetings. For either structure of business, documents must be submitted in Japanese, so it may be necessary to hire a *shihō shoshi* (judicial scrivener) or a *gyōsei shoshi* (administrative scrivener) to handle the process. I-BAC provides free support services.

See **Programs** page **56**

Nagoya Castle Hommaru Palace – Nagoya, Japan

Opening a Bank Account

Several banks don't allow people who have been in Japan for less than six months to open an account, but Japan Post has no such requirement. For services in English, try Prestia SMBC, Seven Bank or Shinsei. While some banks still require a *hanko* (personal seal) to open an account, in general, you will just need your *zairyū* (residence) card, *jūminhyō* (certificate of residence) and a phone number. *Futsū yokin* (general accounts) are the most common and come with a card that enables you to make cash withdrawals from ATMs. Debit cards are rare. ATMs are ubiquitous, but you'll be charged for making a withdrawal from a machine that is not owned by your own bank or if you're withdrawing cash after business hours or during holidays. Online transfers will only be processed during banking business hours. Opening a corporate bank account can be harder and might require speaking with several banks. An introduction through JETRO or I-BAC will help make the process smoother.

See **Banks** page **192**

Taxes

A company that has its main office in Japan is considered resident and will be taxed on its worldwide income. The effective tax rate comes to approximately 30 percent. Aichi Prefecture operates a Business Facility Investment Tax Incentive that may qualify some companies for real estate acquisition tax exemption and reduction, in addition to specific subsidies for foreign companies towards office rent. Individuals pay a progressive income tax, which is capped at 45 percent. Freelancers and the self-employed must file their taxes by the end of March each year, either at their local ward office or online through the e-Tax system (**e-tax.nta.go.jp**). Be prepared for the Residence Tax, which varies depending on your area and your income the previous year. Finding a bilingual accountant will ease the process, and local ward offices offer free assistance during the tax filing season. JETRO can also provide advice on handling taxes.

See **Financial Services** page **193**

Banshoji – Nagoya, Japan

Phone and Internet

Most smartphone users are signed up with a major network provider: Docomo, au or Softbank. All three offer handset-plus-SIM-card deals, typically on two-year contracts, which entail cancellation fees and can cost upwards of ¥10,000 per month depending on the package. However, MVNO (mobile virtual network operators) are on the rise in Japan, offering SIM-only plans for as little as ¥1,400 per month. Few of these offer unlimited calls, and rates are around ¥20 per thirty seconds. For home internet, both ADSL and the faster fiber-optic cable are widely available, although the building in which you live may affect your options. So-Net, NTT and au are among the largest providers. Set up can take two to four weeks, and you'll need to rent a router if you don't have one. Those not wanting to commit to a one- or two-year contract can opt for pocket wifi, which is slower and may have limited data use but has the added bonus of portability. AsahiNet has this option, alongside fiber-optic line connections, and offers full support in English.

Getting Around

Nagoya has an efficient subway system, with one-way fares ranging from ¥210 to ¥340. There is also an extensive bus network, which operates a flat-rate fare of ¥210 during the day and ¥420 for late-night services. If you regularly use the same route, you can buy a *teikiken* (commuter pass), which allows unlimited travel between two stations for a set period. On Saturdays, Sundays, holidays and the eighth day of every month, you can get a one-day pass valid for all city buses and subways for ¥620. Rechargeable contactless cards such as Manaca and TOICA allow quick entry at the ticket gates and can also be used to pay at some shops. Local firm Fuji Taxi has partnered with Uber, but taxis are also easily hailed in the street. The city is well connected to surrounding regions by several train lines, including the Tokaido bullet train, and it is only thirty minutes from Central Japan International Airport by train.

Nagoya, Japan

Learning the Language

You might initially be perplexed by how even ordering a beer in Japanese can earn you effusive praise, but Japanese is notoriously difficult to master. Not only are there two alphabets, but learners must contend with around three thousand *kanji* (Chinese characters), each of which has two or more pronunciations, in addition to honorific and humble language. Japanese pronunciation, however, is simple, and so daily conversation skills are relatively easy to acquire. There is a multitude of flashcard apps to help with kanji memorization. Download a dictionary app that allows a handwriting function for looking up characters. Google Translate also has a camera function for autotranslation of whatever you're looking at. Several schools, including **Nagoya YWCA**, teach a range of courses from general classes to intensive programs. If your budget allows, consider taking private lessons – teachers often offer a free trial lesson, so try out a couple before making a decision.

See **Language Schools** page **193**

Meeting People

Nagoya is close to major urban hubs, the sea, hot springs and mountains, meaning you will never be short of something to do. It's even within easy reach of ski resorts in the winter. There are many Nagoya groups on **meetup.com**, so search for one that matches your interests. Joining coworking spaces is a great way to rapidly embed into a community and share ideas. In July 2019, the Central Japan Economic Foundation and Nagoya City launched **Nagoya Innovator's Garage** to further entrepreneurial collaboration through communal spaces, social nights, academic nights for industry–academia collaboration and mentoring through the Innovator's Garage Entrepreneurs' Society. Not long after, **Nagono Campus** launched in a converted elementary school, providing a coworking space and events. **Nagoya Connect**, powered by **Venture Café Tokyo**, is a free event held on the fourth Friday of every month, spanning everything from panel sessions and workshops to networking opportunities.

See **Groups and Meetups** page **192** and **Startup Events** page **194**

start

ups

[Name]

Craif

[Elevator Pitch]

"Our mission is to detect cancer in the earliest stages using urine. Our core technology is a unique nanowire device that is capable of extracting 99 percent of exosomes, known as promising biomarkers for their deep relationship with diseases."

[The Story]

Ryuichi Onose, CEO and cofounder of Craif, was working at Mitsubishi while both of his grandparents were suffering from cancer. This experience inspired him to move his efforts to improving cancer patients' lives. Venture capital firm ANRI introduced him to Takao Yasui, an associate professor at Nagoya University who was working on developing nanofabrication technologies for biological applications. One promising use of the technology is a liquid biopsy, a method for detecting cancer from body fluids such as blood and urine. Ryuichi and Takao met in March 2018 and cofounded Icaria, later renamed Craif, to bring their technology to market.

The technology provided by Craif enables the measurement of exosomes from a single drop of urine, allowing early cancer detection. It also has the potential to indicate the optimal treatment for each patient, despite the complexity of cancer's pathology. Craif leverages nanomaterial technologies, an area where Japan shows a competitive edge globally, to address one of the world's most significant medical issues.

[Funding History]

Seed   External

Craif received seed funding from ANRI and the Japan Science and Technology Agency. It closed its Series A funding round in June 2020 with investment from ANRI, Daiwa Corporate Investment, Aflac Ventures LLC, Mori Trust, FF APAC Scout and others.

[Milestones]

- Industrializing our nanowire device.
- Receiving validation of the capability to detect cancer in clinical studies.
- Gaining regulatory approval for our device.
- Establishing a base in the US to break into that market

[Links]   Web: craif.com

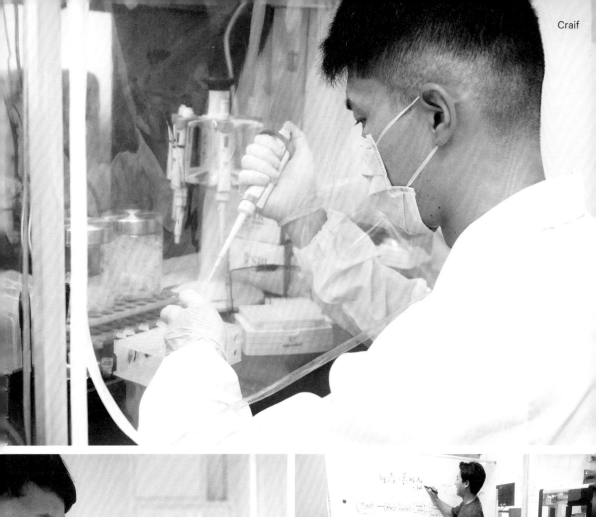

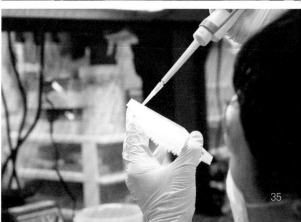

[Name] # GRA&GREEN

[Elevator Pitch] *"We develop technology enabling the rapid creation of new crop varieties, improving taste, disease resistance and growth speed. We provide grafting services and develop and sell grafting cassettes, making it easy to graft vegetable seedlings."*

[The Story] Masaki Niwa and Michitaka Notaguchi started GRA&GREEN in 2017, with an intention to maximize agricultural productivity and sustainability using technology developed at Nagoya University. Masaki, cofounder and CEO, says, "Various issues surround the food and agriculture field, such as climate change, population growth, the shortage of farmers and the need to diversify food."

One technique that can help address such issues is grafting, an ancient method of connecting two different plants to produce a crop that is more resilient, disease resistant or quicker to fruit. But stable production of grafted seedlings is difficult and requires highly skilled workers. To improve the rate of success, GRA&GREEN developed its grafting cassette, a device that enables anyone to mass-produce consistent grafted seedlings. The company also utilizes proprietary technologies, such as gene editing, to combine different plants and create new traits in seedlings. GRA&GREEN aims to build a new agro-food value chain based on contract farming. Masaki says, "This would improve agricultural productivity and contribute to a sustainable society by maximizing the potential of plants through advanced technology."

[Funding History]

Seed   Angel   External

Upon launching in 2017, GRA&GREEN raised several million dollars in seed money via angel investment and funds from Japan Finance Company. It received an additional $2.5 million of Series A funding in February 2020 from Beyond Next Ventures and Sompo Holdings.

[Milestones]
- Founding the company in 2017.
- Raising seed money.
- Successfully developing a viable grafting cassette for market.
- Securing Series A funding.

[Links] Web: **gragreen.com**

[Name] # iBody

[Elevator Pitch] *"Our technology comprehensively and quickly acquires antibodies and creates drugs that have never been seen before. We use it to develop new and innovative therapies for diseases in which autoantibodies are involved, such as cancer and autoimmune diseases."*

[The Story] iBody was founded in February 2018 to commercialize technology developed by Professor Hideo Nakano of Nagoya University's Graduate School of Bioagricultural Sciences. The company uses a core technology called Ecobody, which enables rapid monoclonal antibody discovery and evaluation from single B cells. Conventional antibody drugs are produced against a target such as a molecule or protein specific to a cancer, but they do not work for all people. iBody takes a different approach – it uses Ecobody to take a comprehensive and rapid sample from antibody-producing cells in the body to find antibodies that are most effective on the disease and develops drugs based on them.

The company has plans to further develop its technology and grow. It is focused on acquiring even more effective antibodies to provide better data to the pharmaceutical industry and hopes to further develop its technology through collaboration or joint research with companies.

[Funding History]

External

iBody raised ¥100 million from Nissay Capital in May 2018. In the first half of 2020, it raised a further ¥150 million from Nissay Capital, OKB Capital and Juroku Lease.

[Milestones]
- Founding the company in February 2018.
- Establishing practical uses for Ecobody technology to treat cancer.
- Successfully obtaining promising antibodies that are potential candidates for therapeutic drug development projects.
- Collaborating with different university hospitals on projects for stomach cancer, breast cancer and colorectal cancer.

[Links] Web: **ibody.co.jp**

[Name]
i Smart Technologies

[Elevator Pitch] *"We specialize in IoT systems and services that collect and analyze data to improve the output of factories."*

[The Story] i Smart Technologies was born in 2016 and is dedicated to the development of IoT systems for the manufacturing industry. It started out as a project at Asahi Tekko, an auto-parts manufacturer, and went on to develop a system that later became known as iXacs. The genius behind iXacs is a combination of sensors and software that can continuously capture data by applying devices externally to older machines. It provides new life for aging factories and equipment by optimizing their output. The initial IoT system achieved an average productivity increase of 43 percent across one hundred lines and a cost savings of ¥300 million. i Smart Technologies' focus is on *kaizen*, a Japanese business philosophy that emphasizes continuous improvement and efficiency in both processes and logistics. The goal is to prioritize the acquisition of relevant data and continuously increase productivity step by step, utilizing the client's existing hardware. Management of all data occurs in the cloud, and there is no server or LAN installation required.

Today, iXacs is a service that combines hardware and software along with extensive support. Until now, many small and medium-sized companies could not afford the capital investment required to enter the realm of IoT, but i Smart Technologies' service is relevant to a broad market due to the low cost of implementation and the resulting savings.

[Funding History]

Seed

i Smart Technologies is a spin-off of Asahi Tekko, which has loaned it a total of ¥200 million. Currently, it relies on revenue and is not seeking outside funding.

[Milestones]
- Beginning the development of the iXacs system at Asahi Tekko in 2014.
- Establishing i Smart Technologies as a separate company in 2016.
- Beginning promotional activities in Ishikawa Prefecture in 2018.
- Releasing an enhanced version of services in 2019.

[Links] Web: **istc.co.jp** Facebook: **I-Smart-Technologies-787846324724275**

[Name]
Optimind

[Elevator Pitch]
"We created the Loogia route-optimization service for last-mile delivery operators. Our AI calculates which vehicles should go to which destinations, in what order and on what routes, automating the complexities of efficient delivery for dispatchers."

[The Story]
As a freshman at Nagoya University, Optimind's president and CEO Ken Matsushita came across the concept of combinatorial optimization and was impressed by its utility. Combinatorial optimization uses combinatorial methods to solve optimization problems and determine the best result from a fixed set of probabilities. Ken focused his studies on the method and contemplated how it could be used in technological applications. In 2015, he created Optimind to optimize distribution routes.

Optimind's Loogia platform is a cloud-based route-optimization service that is used by last-mile delivery businesses and wholesalers. The company's proprietary algorithms analyze GPS data collected from drivers and calculate the optimal dispatch and delivery paths for each package. With this technology, Optimind has realized an efficient delivery system and helped its customers become more profitable by reducing delivery times and delays. "Optimind's primary customers are involved in home delivery, such as Japan Post and Nitori," Ken says. "Another customer category is liquor wholesalers that sell beer and meat to restaurants. Construction companies also utilize our services, delivering water valves and building materials to construction sites. So basically, we are involved in home delivery and wholsale delivery."

[Funding History]

Seed   External

In 2018, Optimind raised ¥100 million in seed funding from Warehouse Terada and Tier IV. In October 2019, it secured ¥1.3 billion in Series A funding with Toyota Motor as the lead investor and investment from Mitsubishi, KDDI and MTG Ventures.

[Milestones]
- Developing an accurate algorithm that is effective in real-world applications.
- Improving the ability of the service to accurately estimate route speed via GPS.
- Releasing Loogia to customers.
- Establishing a customer base exceeding seventy clients.

[Links]   Web: **optimind.tech** Facebook: **optimindloogia** Twitter: **@optimind_pr**

[Name] # Prodrone

[Elevator Pitch] *"We develop, manufacture and provide industrial drones. We are working to develop specialized drones as a service, including their operation and software."*

[The Story] In 2014, founder and chairman Masakazu Kono was working for System Five, a professional broadcasting equipment company, when he received an inquiry from a customer about obtaining a drone. It was intended to be a one-off project, but Masakazu was inspired by the drone industry's possibilities. He contacted friends in the engineering and software fields to work with him, and Prodrone was born. The company began by manufacturing custom-engineered industrial drones developed to customer requirements. In Japan, there are various laws and regulations that must be followed to operate drones, and deregulation was moving slowly during Prodrone's initial startup, causing hurdles in business development. The company has lobbied for easier operating rules and works to raise public awareness of the issue.

Masakazu says that he has gathered his "dream team" and believes that his company "has it all": patents, hardware design, flight control software and the drone pilot. He says that "without these five things, industrial drones are hard to fly. The one thing that's important is that we've been able to do things that other companies couldn't do." Prodrone ultimately plans to launch a complete service that includes the creation of specialized drones for clients, as well as operation and maintenance.

[Funding History]

Seed   External

In 2016, Prodrone completed its first round of funding, receiving investment from several major companies. It undertook a second round in 2018, and to date has raised ¥1.7 billion.

[Milestones]
- Launching in January 2015.
- Completing our first round of investment in 2016.
- Founder Masakazu Kono winning the Grand Prize in the Challenging Spirit category at the Entrepreneur of the Year 2017 Japan Awards (EOY Japan).
- Being awarded the Patent Office Commissioner's Award by the Ministry of Economy, Trade and Industry, a first in the drone industry.

[Links] Web: **prodrone.com** Facebook: **Prodrone-Inc-757970477704777** Twitter: **@prodronecom**

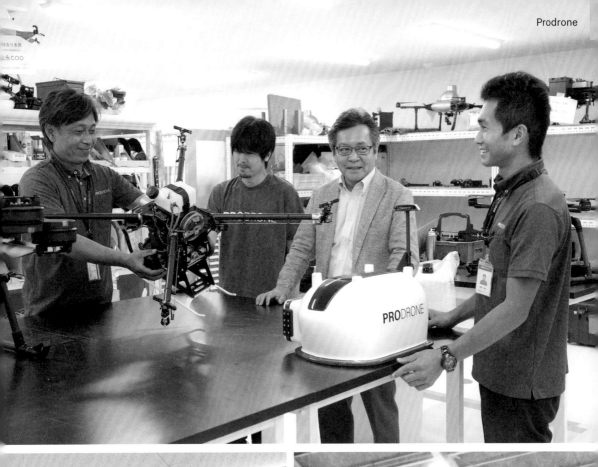

[Name] # stmn

[Elevator Pitch] *"We are a company where both people and organizations win. We create products that strengthen relationships, helping our clients gain a competitive advantage through engaging their employees."*

[The Story] stmn was founded in 2016 with the vision of creating a platform service that utilizes technology to improve the connection between companies and their employees. Its focus is on employee retention, the reduction of recruitment costs and improving business performance. stmn's initial product, TUNAG, is an engagement-management platform and service that is tailored to each company's specific needs.

TUNAG is a continuous, data-driven consulting service that harnesses know-how derived from the analysis of over three thousand internal systems. It facilitates communication among employees as well as between employees and management to advance a culture of praise. TUNAG promotes a positive workplace using a system built around internal networks and a timeline that identifies the initiatives and day-to-day activities of various departments within the company. It includes organizational charts, a chat function, a point system that offers rewards, virtual thank you cards, file sharing and workflow systems, among other features. Additionally, it provides engagement assessments that identify organizational challenges utilizing proprietary criteria. stmn's aim is that TUNAG will help its users reduce the gap between management and employees.

[Funding History]

Seed   Angel   External

stmn began developing TUNAG in August 2016. It received ¥280 million of equity in March 2017 from JAFCO, Chukyo TV, DG Ventures and angel investors.

[Milestones]
- Releasing TUNAG in April 2017.
- Being named one of the 100 Amazing Ventures in *Toyo Kezai* magazine in 2019.
- Being named Startup Architecture of the Year 2019 by Amazon Web Services.
- Being ranked as the greatest place to work in Japan by Great Place to Work Institute Japan

[Links] Web: **stmn.co.jp** LinkedIn: **company/stmninc.** Facebook: **stmn.co.jp** Instagram: **stmn_inc** Twitter: **@tunag_stmn**

[Name] # Tier IV

[Elevator Pitch] *"We create an autonomous-driving platform based on Autoware, the world's first open-source software for autonomous driving. We offer a wide range of integration services using our autonomous-driving platform for mobility and logistics applications."*

[The Story] Tier IV's founder and CTO Shinpei Kato created the company when he was an associate professor in the Graduate School of Information Science at Nagoya University. Professor Kazuya Takeda, who now serves as president of Tier IV, supported Shinpei in his research on open-source software for autonomous driving. The model that he developed received so much attention that Shinpei decided to develop it as a venture, launching Tier IV in December 2015. The concept of open-source software for autonomous driving is appealing to automotive companies both domestically and abroad because it is challenging to create such technology from scratch. Several such companies came to Tier IV to customize the software for their products.

Tier IV's goal is to create intelligent vehicles for everyone. Through Autoware, the world's first open-source software for autonomous driving, the company aims to build an ecosystem of global partners worldwide that contribute to autonomous-driving technology. True to his goal of making the software open and accessible, Shinpei transferred all rights to Tier IV's technology to the nonprofit Autoware Foundation.

[Funding History]

Bootstrap   Seed   Angel   External

Tier IV was initially bootstrapped. In July 2019, the company raised over ¥11 billion in Series A funding from Sompo Japan Insurance, Yamaha Motor, KDDI, JAFCO and Aisan Technology. In September 2020, it announced that it had raised additional funding from Sompo Holdings, taking its total funding to ¥17.5 billion.

[Milestones]
- Establishing the company in 2015.
- Conducting the first testing of self-driving cars on Japanese public roads.
- Establishing the nonprofit organization Autoware Foundation.
- Delivering completed guaranteed products for the Tokyo 2020 version of Toyota e-Palette.

[Links] Web: **tier4.jp** LinkedIn: **company/tier-iv-inc** Facebook: **TierIV**
Instagram: **tier_iv** Twitter: **@tier_iv_japan**

[Name] # TOWING

[Elevator Pitch] *"Our mission is to expand where humans can live and create solutions for food-production challenges. We are developing technology to enable food production in space, as well as tackling agriculture problems on Earth, such as land degradation and food demand."*

[The Story] TOWING was founded in February 2020 by two brothers, CEO Kohei Nishida and COO and CTO Ryoya Nishida. The company develops highly productive food-cultivation systems for locations where growing food is either difficult or expensive. In recent years, many companies have attempted to create and implement resource-recycling cultivation systems but found them to be expensive and time consuming to develop. TOWING's technology uses a proprietary algorithm to determine what types of artificial soil and organic fertilizer are appropriate for each location. Its approach dramatically shortens the setup period for optimizing the soil environment.

The company aims to expand its system to Europe and North America, where organic food markets are mature. The technology also has an application in developing countries, where demand for food is rapidly growing in relation to expanding populations, as it allows food production in harsh environments such as deserts and alpine regions. As part of the SPACE FOODSPHERE program, a Tokyo-based initiative, TOWING is working on ways to cultivate food on the International Space Station, the moon and Mars.

[Funding History]

Seed   External

TOWING raised its initial seed capital of approximately $10,000 through prize money from business contests. It is about to enter its first external funding round.

[Milestones]
- Developing a system of cultivating food utilizing artificial soil combined with a unique algorithm to optimize the production of food under a variety of conditions.
- Gathering business partners.
- Joining the SPACE FOODSPHERE program in August 2020.
- Initializing plans to disseminate our technology abroad.

[Links] Web: **towing.co.jp** Facebook: **towing.sorano**

[Name] # TRYETING

[Elevator Pitch] *"We can quickly, cheaply and effectively make our clients' systems intelligent using AaaS. We provide cost-reducing, AI-driven services such as efficient inventory management and shift optimization to a wide range of companies."*

[The Story] TRYETING is currently one of a few companies in Japan that offer AI-enabled platforms to extract and manipulate data. Its goals are to use data relevant to each customer's specific needs and to improve productivity by eliminating tasks needlessly done by humans, saving time and money and allowing employees to focus on more important tasks. TRYETING's customers include major car-parts manufacturers and clothing distributors, both of which manage large inventories. The company is increasingly looking into the wellness sector and working on wearable devices that continuously assess human health.

TRYETING has developed several sophisticated algorithms geared towards machine learning and aspires to optimize its systems to make them more efficient, faster and bigger. To do this, it is making strides with edge computing on location and utilizing quantum computing to process big data. It aims to render the input data lighter, thus saving the amount of time it takes to send it to cloud servers for parallel computing. The plan is to use the resulting data from the cloud to train the model and create a new algorithm to control local edge devices. This middle environment between cloud computing and edge servers is called "fog computing." With this kind of AI system, the data transfer is much faster than in traditional systems.

[Funding History]

Bootstrap   Seed   Angel

TRYETING was initially bootstrapped through sales. It closed a Series A funding round in August 2019 with approximately ¥300 million. In October 2019, the company closed a Series A extension round. Its primary funding came from Toyoda Gosei, Tokai Tokyo Investment, Shizuoka Capital and angel investors.

[Milestones]
- Launching in June 2016.
- Receiving approximately $3,800,000 in Series A and Series A extension funding in 2019.
- Beginning a collaborative investment with Toyoda Gosei to rapidly develop materials using AI.
- Developing an AI-enabled server (Umwelt) in March 2018.

[Links]   Web: **tryeting.jp** Facebook: **Tryeting** Twitter: **@Tryetingoficial**

[Name] # United Immunity

[Elevator Pitch] *"We are a biotech company with a unique approach that combines nanotechnology with immunotherapy to treat cancer. Harmful macrophages are related to the inability to cure cancer, and we focus on them to create an effective treatment."*

[The Story] United Immunity was founded in November 2017 by a research team led by Naozumi Harada, who was based at Mie University. Since 2012, his team has been working with researchers from Kyoto University to develop a technology combining nanotechnology and immunotherapy to treat cancer. They decided to create a business based on the technology, and United Immunity was born. Clinical trials were conducted in spring 2020 while they raised funds.

The technology used by United Immunity is called T-ignite. T cells are essential immune cells that help fight cancer. Antibody drugs that energize patients' T cells are already used in the treatment of cancer. However, harmful cells called macrophages can diminish the effectiveness of T cells – in some cases, they stop the T cells from attacking cancer. Dealing with macrophages is difficult, but research has shown that it may be possible to utilize nanoparticles to deliver drugs to the macrophages inside cancerous tissue to inhibit their function, and this is where United Immunity is focusing its efforts. T-ignite is United Immunity's most advanced program, but it also has several other products involving nanotechnology in the pipeline.

[Funding History]

Seed　　　　　Angel　　　　　External

During its seed phase, United Immunity raised ¥30 million from KISCO and DG Ventures. Series A funding took place from March to June 2019 and raised ¥60 million from Mitsubishi UFJ Capital and Axil Capital. The company also raised about ¥10 million from individual shareholders between 2017 and 2019.

[Milestones]
- Completing the first stage of clinical trials, with good results.
- Signing an agreement that allows us to use the intellectual property currently owned by Mie University and Kyoto University.
- Receiving government funding of ¥300 million for the development of a nanoparticle vaccine to prevent COVID-19.
- Entering talks regarding a program with a world-renowned farmer.

[Links]　Web: unitedimmunity.co.jp

- **Rethink your abilities.**
  What skills and networks have you developed?
  If you are an employee, what are the company's and
  your core skills? Knowing your own abilities will be an
  asset in this program.

- **Don't be afraid of failure.**
  Failing is learning. Try first, and if you fail, analyze
  and develop a new direction. It's essential to try.

- **Think big.**
  Picture what you want to change. Put your thoughts
  into trying to realize it from a broad perspective.
  Having a long-term vision will help you identify a goal
  in the program.

- **Stand out and disrupt.**
  Half-hearted thoughts can crush you. Are you ready
  to break out of your shell? Are you willing to buck
  conventional wisdom?

[Name]

Beyond the Border

[Elevator Pitch]

"We foster innovation drivers who strongly promote the creation of new value through understanding and deepening common technologies, the concept of future society and cocreation through fusion of different fields. Beyond the Border is a program to connect."

[Sector] **Sector-agnostic**

[Description] Beyond the Border is a six-month, twelve-part program for entrepreneurial development based on collaboration and cocreation. Created by Nagoya Innovator's Garage, it is open to anyone up to around the age of thirty-five who has an interest in tech-enabled entrepreneurship or in developing skills to take back to their company. A wide range of people have taken part, including representatives from many different industries in the region. The program organizers also encourage university students to participate. One of the unique features of this program is its focus on forming networks among people from different backgrounds.

The program is divided into three steps and starts with an introductory session on the mindset of business creation. The first step is Knowledge Stretch, in which participants learn about technologies relevant to creating new businesses, such as AI, IoT and robotics. Students learn how to innovate and utilize their company's core technology or their own existing knowledge in new ways. The second step is Future Design, in which participants gain real-world experience through fieldwork and site visits. They also learn how to identify social issues in daily life and envision potential solutions by looking at future technologies. Finally, in Business Co-Creation, participants work in groups to develop a business plan and propose solutions to social issues by utilizing the different core competencies and technologies of team members from different fields and with practical guidance from a facilitator. The goal is to create new value.

The program includes lectures from industry experts, including seasoned entrepreneurs, technology professors and economists. It is made up of twelve parts and costs a total of ¥300,000. After the program, graduates continue to have access to mentors and experts to further develop their concepts. Members of the first cohort have launched MIXUP, a service that connects people providing pro bono services with small businesses.

[Apply to] **beyond@garage-nagoya.or.jp**

[Links] Web: **garage-nagoya.or.jp/program/p3144** Facebook: **nagoyainnovatorsgarage**

- **Demonstrate a desire to learn new skills.**
  This opportunity is for people to think about open innovation, new business creation, entrepreneurship and skills improvement.

- **Show a desire to participate in the program.**
  Be ready to stick it out. We are looking for participants who have the determination to complete the program.

- **Take the know-how and use it.**
  Whether you want to start a business or are already working for a company, we want you to learn new ideas and make something of them.

- **Don't just sit down and learn.**
  We have a mentorship program, and we want you to learn from others to increase your output. We try to provide companionship and support to encourage you.

[Name] # NAGOYA BOOST 10000

[Elevator Pitch] *"We're a program originally designed to create ten thousand entrepreneurs and business creators in this region. We organize a hackathon and an AI and IoT talent development program, as well as pitch events."*

[Sector] AI, IoT

[Description] NAGOYA BOOST 10000 is an innovator training and business creation program from Nagoya City and based out of Nagoya Innovator's Garage that is intended to hone technology skills and nurture aspiring entrepreneurs. It has three components: Nagoya Hackathon, the AI/IoT Human Resource BOOST program and Nagoya BOOST DAY. Nagoya Hackathon promotes collaboration across industries and aims to discover new business ideas using the latest technology. Each year, the hackathon has a specific theme, with 2020's event aimed at finding new value in a world changed by COVID-19.

The AI/IoT Human Resource BOOST Program is intended for people who want to start a business or develop an idea but don't know where to begin. Representatives from small, medium and large companies have attended the six-month course and used the skills learned to create new concepts within their organizations. Individual participants including college students are also welcome and collaboration among people from different backgrounds is encouraged. The program teaches prototyping technologies in AI and IoT, 3D CAD and chassis prototyping and business development skills such as accounting, marketing and understanding of intellectual property. It has a focus on "output-type new business creation," which organizers say improves the accuracy of output in a short period of time through user evaluation and the repeating of input and output. Participants are also required to complete a presentation skills course to help them prepare for pitch events.

Nagoya BOOST DAY is an event where participants from both the hackathon and the AI/IoT Human Resource BOOST Program can present their projects to the wider community. Notable local startups that have participated in NAGOYA BOOST 10000 include LINK, a long-term care service, and agtech startup TOWING.

[Apply to] a3046@keizai.city.nagoya.lg.jp

[Links] Web: nagoyaboost.jp Facebook: groups/nagoyaboost10000

- **Have an interest in learning about ICT.**
  We look for SMEs that want to create new value by
  combining their strengths with the latest technology.
  We don't expect you to have in-depth knowledge
  of ICT, but you should be interested in the field
  and familiar with its basic concepts.

- **Show motivation to create and expand your business.**
  We look for people who are motivated to create
  a new business or expand an existing one.

- **Show the ability to implement.**
  Do you have the management skills and the
  commitment to implement a business plan?
  Can you follow through?

[Name] # Nagoya ICT Innovation Lab

[Elevator Pitch] *"We support the creation of new businesses and products by combining the resources of entrepreneurs and small and medium-sized companies with the latest ICT technology."*

[Sector] **Information and communications technology**

[Description] Nagoya ICT Innovation Lab is a program provided by Nagoya Mirai Innovators with an aim of enhancing Nagoya's industrial and technological base. Established in 2019 by Nagoya City, it supports small and medium-sized enterprises in creating new products, services and businesses that address societal challenges by leveraging participants' strengths and technology. Participants are often small and medium-sized businesses that want to add value to their company by incorporating technologies. However, even organizations that have no human resources or knowledge of ICT but possess a strong desire to participate can enroll.

The program accepts roughly forty people from up to twenty companies in each cohort, with one or two participants from each company. The content is based around problem solving, idea development, testing hypotheses and learning how to create prototypes. It combines classroom-based lessons and lectures with practical learning, including workshops, meetings with experts and mentoring. Startups to come out of Nagoya ICT Innovation Lab include iHACCP, which combines IoT technology with HACCP to create a system that controls temperatures in restaurants.

Nagoya Mirai Innovators also offers the Nagoya Women Startup Lab, which is open to women aiming to start a business in Nagoya and female founders with a business less than five years old. The program accepts approximately fifteen people into each cohort and is based around four seminars. It helps participants to create and develop business plans and conduct market research. It also supports initiatives by providing the opportunity to participate in exhibitions held in Nagoya and Tokyo, and by connecting participants with its network of established entrepreneurs.

[Apply to] a2417@keizai.city.nagoya.lg.jp

[Links] Web: nagoya-innovation.jp/nagoya-mirai Facebook: 758ictinnovation

- **Be based in the Tokai region.**
  Our primary motivation is to build a startup ecosystem from the Tokai region, although we offer many online programs that can be taken by people from all over Japan.

- **Show an interest in testing ideas.**
  Tongali starts from the bottom up. The main goal is to bring together people who want to challenge themselves. You may not have a clear idea, but we want people who are open to possibilities.

- **Be interested in learning.**
  We want to cultivate people, and we want to empower them to build their startups.

- **Focus on the positive.**
  One of the main features of the Tongali program is that it is constructive, not critical. We aim to provide a safe environment for people to challenge themselves.

[Name]

Tongali Project

[Elevator Pitch]

"We are an entrepreneurship education program for students and graduates. We offer a system that teaches participants how to start a business and provide access to mentors, who offer direct guidance."

[Sector]

Sector-agnostic

[Description]

The Tongali Project was launched in 2016 and is a collaborative venture created by five universities in the Tokai region. The project's aims are to develop future innovators and entrepreneurs to contribute to the revitalization of industry and job creation in the Tokai region and to build a global innovation ecosystem. It does this through providing mentoring, training, financial support, coworking space and events. The Tongali Program targets undergraduate and graduate students, postdoctoral fellows, faculty members and graduates in the Tokai region, and also supports university-launched ventures. It is sector-agnostic in the ventures it supports but has a focus on deeptech.

The project's main program is the Seminar/Education Program, which is free to join. The symposium is intended for people who aren't sure if they want to start their own business or not. Participants are encouraged to undertake a series of steps, the first of which is developing an entrepreneurial mindset. Attendees participate in a workshop called Tongali School, where they learn about frameworks such as design thinking and creating an advanced business model. There are also options to take courses online. The culmination of the program is a business plan contest, at which the winner receives funding and mentoring to make their business concept a reality.

[Apply to]

tongali.net

[Links]

Web: **tongali.net** Facebook: **Nagoya.Univ.info.tongali** Twitter: **@NU_Tongali**

ces

Meijo University Social Collaboration Zone Shake

[Name]

[Address] 4-102-9 Yadaminami, Higashi-ku, Nagoya 461-8534

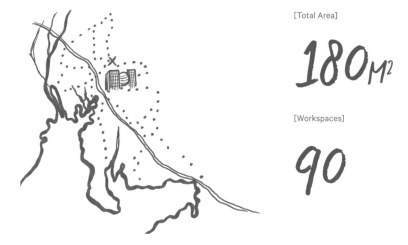

[Total Area]

*180*M²

[Workspaces]

90

[The Story] Before Meijo University built a new campus in 2016, Nagoya didn't have many spaces where students, faculty, business people and entrepreneurs could connect. That is why the university created Social Collaboration Zone Shake (also known as Shake), a coworking space that anyone can use without a reservation. The space is bright and airy, and was modeled after a similar facility at Stanford University. There are four main zones: the Idea Exchange Space is where people can collaborate and converse; the Dialogue Space is a comfortable place to bounce ideas off each other; in the Working Space, there are desks and a whiteboard to allow people to immerse themselves in group or individual work; and the Project Room is a base for project activities. There is also a large multiscreen LCD panel and an electronic blackboard to make presentations and discussions easier.

Since Shake opened, its partnerships have grown to more than 140, including many groups working within the university. A diverse range of students and faculty from the university and other educational institutions, as well as businesses and government entities, use the space.

[Links] Web: plat.meijo-u.ac.jp/shake Facebook: meijoshake Instagram: plat_mj Twitter: @meijoPLAT

Face of the Space:
Masashi Kato is a professor of agriculture and the head of the Center for Social Cooperation and Partnership, which runs Shake. Gouki Yamamoto works for the Center for Social Cooperation and Partnership and has overseen Shake's operations since its launch. Chisa Miyahara is a coordinator, and her role includes connecting people who want to use Shake with the university and organizing seminars.

[Name] # Midland Incubators House

[Address] Room 142, Shin Nagoya Center Building, Honjin-gai,
1-1 Ibukacho, Nakamura-ku, Nagoya 453-0012

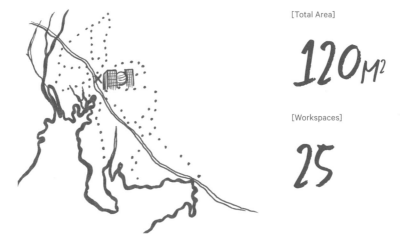

[Total Area]

120M²

[Workspaces]

25

[The Story]   Located under the Shinkansen railway tracks near Kamejima Station, Midland Incubators House was founded in June 2018 by Kenta Okumura and Ryuichiro Toyoshi. The two men are behind the successful startup Misoca and wanted to share their knowledge and experience to expand the ecosystem in the central Japan region. Midland Incubators House is free to use and intended to be a space where entrepreneurs, potential entrepreneurs and others can gather and collaborate. There is a general understanding that Nagoya's business community is closed, a notion that Kenta and Ryuichiro would like to change. The organization aims to increase the number of entrepreneurs in the area by providing support through free space, events and investment.

Midland Incubators House has a focus on supporting young aspiring entrepreneurs, and its U29 meetups target this demographic. The space also hosts events for middle and high school students who want to become entrepreneurs, as well as twenty-minute Speed Meetups and other events. Most of the people who work from the space are involved in IT in some capacity, though their application of technology is varied. There are members working in healthtech, human resources, cosmetics and more.

[Links]   Web: m15s.jp Facebook: Midland.Incubators Twitter: @Mid_Incubators

Face of the Space:
Ryuichiro Toyoshi graduated from Gifu
National College of Technology before
founding Misoca, a cloud-based invoicing
and management service, in 2011.
Kenta Okumura graduated from Kyoto
University and then joined Misoca in
2014, ultimately becoming the executive
officer in charge of financial strategy.
Both eventually left Misoca to found
Midland Incubators House.

[Name] # MUSASHi Innovation Lab CLUE

[Address]   Cocola Avenue 3F, 1-135 Ekimae Odori, Toyohashi 440-0888

[Total Area]

237m²

[Workspaces]

40

[The Story]   MUSASHi Innovation Lab CLUE (also known just as CLUE) was established in 2018 by Musashi Seimitsu Kogyo, whose primary business is the manufacture and sale of automotive parts. The company's goals were to create an innovation hub and an ecosystem that fosters entrepreneurship within companies and to collaborate with startups to develop innovative technologies and business models that help solve social issues in the East Mikawa region.

The space is conveniently situated in front of the city's central transit hub, Toyohashi Station, and is open from 9 AM to 6 PM on weekdays. An open space located on the third floor of a modern building, it has work booths, a meeting room and a lounge, as well as a small stage for events and presentations. CLUE's organizers say that it provides three Ps: a place where you may forget daily life, people of diversity and a process to generate innovation. The organization offers opportunities to network with entrepreneurs in Japan and elsewhere, connecting members with potential investors and mentors from diverse backgrounds through its events and seminars, many of which are free.

[Links]   Web: musashi.co.jp/clue Facebook: MUSASHi.Innovation.Lab.CLUE
Instagram: musashi.innovation.lab.clue Twitter: @MusashiLab_CLUE

Face of the Space:
Sachiyo Tamaya and Takafumi Suzuki are CLUE's community managers. Sachiyo joined the organization in 2017 and enjoys sharing her startup experience with members. Takafumi enjoys hosting seminars and pitch events for startups and individuals working on new initiatives.

[Name] # Nagoya Innovator's Garage

[Address] Nadya Park 4F, 3-18-1 Sakae, Naka-ku, Nagoya 460-0008

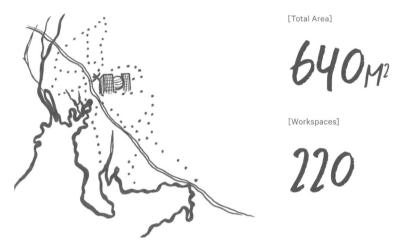

[Total Area]

640M²

[Workspaces]

220

[The Story] The Central Japan Economic Federation established the Innovation Study Group in 2016 and was looking for a place that could serve as an innovation hub for the central Japan region since its foundation. In consultation with Nagoya City, it received a proposal in the spring of 2018 to utilize the International Design Center at Nadya Park in Nagoya's central Sakae district. Nagoya Innovator's Garage opened here in July 2019 as a joint project between Nagoya City and the central Japan business community.

The space offers a number of programs, all with the goal of fusing industry, government and academia, and functions as a hub for innovation activities. The organization aims to promote openness and exchange between people of all ages, genders and nationalities. Anyone interested in starting a business is encouraged to visit the space for support and inspiration. In addition to desks and offices, there is a conference area that can be adapted to accommodate either small or large meetings. Nagoya Innovator's Garage also hosts regular community-building events and lectures, with past activities including speeches from Nobel Prize winners and successful startup founders. Individual membership is ¥60,000 per year.

[Links] Web: garage-nagoya.or.jp Facebook: nagoyainnovatorsgarage
Instagram: nagoya_innovators_garage

Face of the Space:
Director General Hirooki Fujiwara is a
designated professor at the Innovation
Strategy Office of Nagoya University.
As Secretary-General of the Central
Japan Economic Federation, he
encouraged the establishment of Nagoya
Innovator's Garage. Naoki Inagaki works
for Nagoya City, promoting, supporting
and encouraging innovation for startups.
He is in charge of projects related to ICT
and digital content. As a project manager
for Nagoya City, Yuki Goto promotes
next-generation industries and
innovation for SMEs.

[Name] # Nagono Campus

[Address] 2-14-1 Nagono, Nishi-ku, Nagoya 451-0042

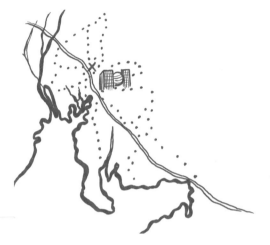

[Total Area]

4,178m²

[Workspaces]

220

[The Story] Nagono Campus incorporates private offices, shared offices and a coworking space. Located in the former Nagono Elementary School, it is conveniently located just eight minutes by foot from Nagoya Station, the city's central transportation hub. The space opened in 2019 and features a gymnasium, an event space, meeting rooms, an outdoor area and a restaurant located in the former school cafeteria. Members of the coworking space and shared offices include startups, freelancers and students, and there is a corporate membership program for large companies.

Members say that they enjoy working from Nagono Campus because of the comfortable environment, the ability to network and because it is affordable. The organization provides consultation on entrepreneurship and business concepts, as well as information about grants and crowdfunding. Seminars, workshops and pitch contests are also regularly held at the facility. The coworking space has a "trouble board" where members can anonymously leave feedback, express their opinions about the space and make suggestions.

[Links] Web: **nagono-campus.jp** Facebook: **nagonocampus** Twitter: **@nagono_campus**

Face of the Space:
Keigo Ito and Yoko Kitahara are both
responsible for sales at Nagono Campus.
Keigo joined the company in April 2017
after graduating from what is now Tokyo
Metropolitan University. Yoko joined
Nagono Campus in 2020. Before this,
she worked at Unizo Holdings, Asahi
Kasei Real Estate Residence and
Hyakusen-Renma.

[Name] # WeWork Global Gate Nagoya

[Address]   4-60-12 Hiraikecho, Nakamura-ku, Nagoya 453-6111

[Floors]

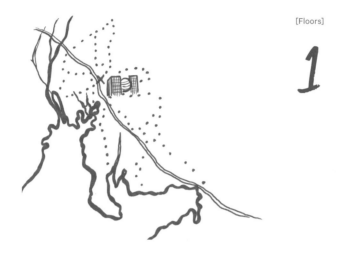

1

[The Story]   WeWork Global Gate Nagoya is located on the eleventh floor of the stylish Global Gate complex, within walking distance of the city's central transport hub, Nagoya Station, and directly linked to Sasashima-raibu Station. The area is the focus of extensive development and boasts a high-end hotel and many restaurants and shops. This winning combination makes it an ideal place for travelers, remote workers and those looking for a community-focused space to work from. Since it opened in 2019, WeWork Global Gate Nagoya has hosted startups, representatives from large companies including PayPay and even government organizations. Aichi Prefecture uses the space as a base to work with local entrepreneurs and holds events here and in other WeWork locations across Japan.

Members can enjoy a variety of events each week, including seminars, happy hours and member-organized get-togethers. In keeping with WeWork's goal of community-building, the space has hosted several online networking events that were attended by members from WeWork locations across the country. As well as hot desks, there are private offices, meeting rooms, phone booths, printing facilities and all-you-can-drink coffee and beer. There's also a meditation room, and the space is located above a yoga studio.

[Links]   Web: wework.com/buildings/global-gate-nagoya--nagoya LinkedIn: company/wework
Facebook: WeWorkJapan Instagram: wework Twitter: @WeWorkJP

Face of the Space:
After graduating from the University
of California, Ken Matsue worked as a
university employee. He then moved into
the apparel industry, where he worked in
in-store operations and human resources
at a major foreign apparel company.
Currently, he works at WeWork Japan as
a community director and is involved in
managing multiple locations, including
WeWork Global Gate Nagoya.

erts

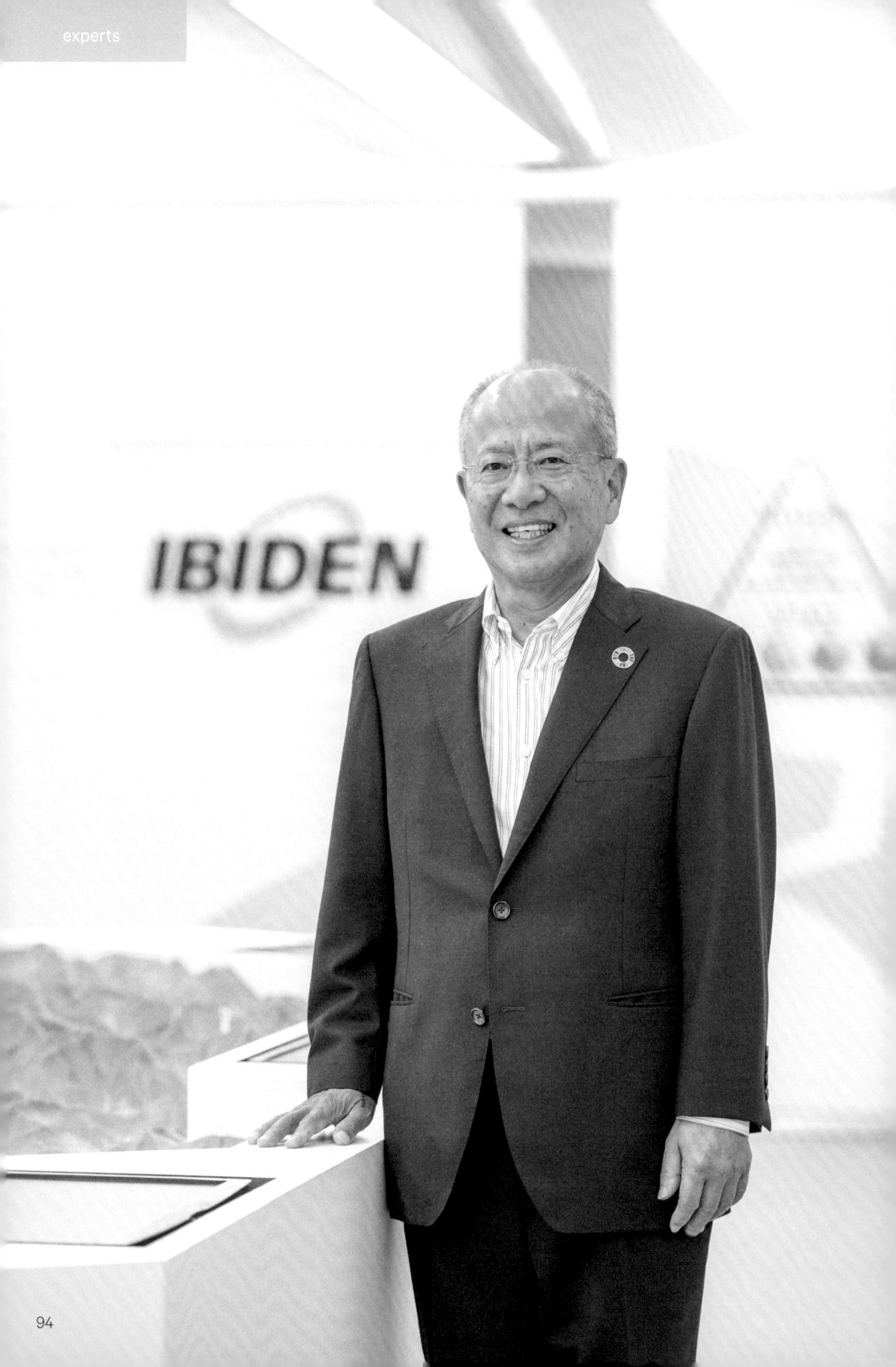
IBIDEN

Fostering Innovation through Outstanding Leadership

Hiroki Takenaka / Chairman and Representative Director at IBIDEN

[Sector] **Electronics, ceramics, building materials, electric power and construction**

At the core of every startup is a leader who can balance commitment and flexibility. "To be successful in a constantly changing world, you need to be able to lead your team to the ultimate goal, even if you sometimes need to change the means of getting there," says Hiroki Takenaka, chairman and representative director of IBIDEN. Mr. Takenaka joined IBIDEN in 1973 and held several leadership positions before becoming president of the company in 2007. Through his career journey, he has gained a wealth of insights on organizational development and business growth in central Japan and around the world.

A true Japanese conglomerate with the spirit of a startup, IBIDEN is constantly developing new products in response to rapidly changing times. From its humble roots in Gifu Prefecture, the company has steadily grown over the last century to become a global powerhouse and an international market leader in various fields including electronics, ceramics, building materials and electric power.

For founders who wish to emulate IBIDEN's success, charismatic leadership is critical. Fortunately, Mr. Takenaka has plenty of advice to share on this topic. "Charismatic leaders are able to partner with customers who appreciate the new products or values they come up with," he says. "Partnerships are the most important aspect of a business-to-business operation. Startups have limited resources and those resources should be focused on core technologies. Anything beyond that should be outsourced to external partners that are specialists."

Founders also need to be excellent communicators. "Typically, startups don't have a lot of time to take their product to market," says Mr. Takenaka. He recommends backcasting, a scheduling method that starts with a desired future outcome and forecasts backward to the present. "Backcasting leaves little time to spare, and usually work is done in parallel by several departments and groups," he says. "During this process, communication with stakeholders such as internal teams, external contractors and customers is essential."

Most important tips for startups:

- **Charismatic leadership is critical.** You need to be able
  to forge partnerships with discerning customers who
  understand and appreciate your products and ideas.

- **Focus on your core technology as you pursue your
  development goals.** Concentrate limited internal resources
  on core technology. Everything else can be outsourced
  as necessary.

- **Rely on backcasting.** Bring your product to market
  on time by scheduling backward from a future deadline.

- **Combine traditional refinement with modern technology.**
  The sweet spot for success in central Japan lies at the
  intersection of high production standards and digital
  technology.

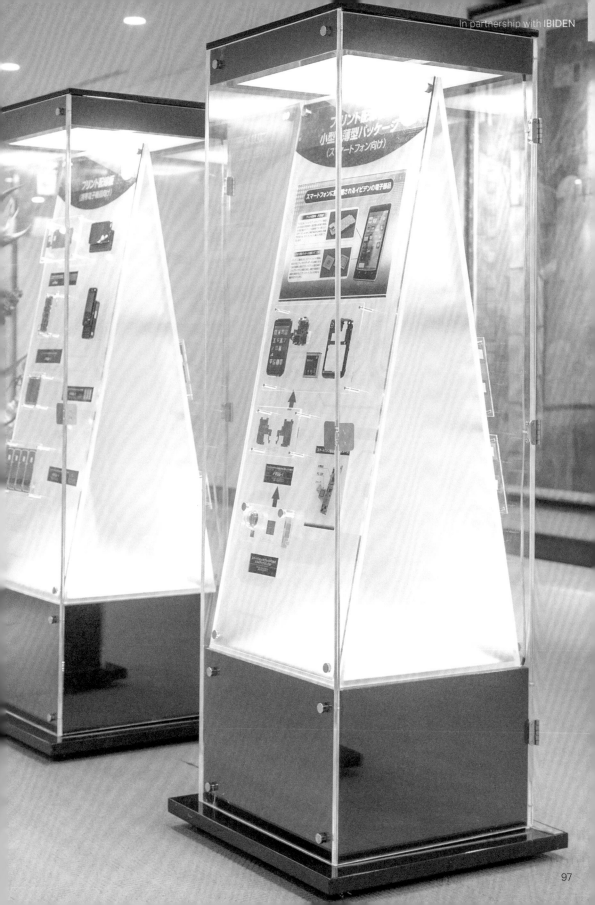

Organizations that move forward in this way can push toward their goals, even if they are forced to reevaluate their plans from time to time. "This means that in order to achieve success, leaders need to constantly visualize the big picture, and they need to be able to accurately convey that visualization to their team," says Mr. Takenaka.

In addition to strategically allocating limited resources and being exceptional communicators, founders need to carefully manage the operations of their fledgling organizations. "New businesses may be too small to cover all functional aspects necessary to run an organization," says Mr. Takenaka. "Rely on external partners to help with any business functions that you can't cover." Additionally, founders shouldn't be afraid of experiencing and learning from failures early on. "As you overcome mistakes, better results will be born," he says. "Failure is a fortune. You can make steady progress while making many small mistakes. Work toward the ultimate goal of overcoming failure and creating something better."

Despite IBIDEN's global presence, Mr. Takenaka is quick to highlight the merits of starting a business in central Japan. "The strength of this region lies in the manufacturing industry," he says. "Companies here take pride in their ability to achieve the highest standards of productivity and quality while keeping total costs low." Mr. Takenaka believes that combining these qualities with modern digital technology will create opportunities for startups. Additionally, businesses in central Japan are influenced by the region's geography. "Surrounded by the sea and mountains, we are blessed with an environment that is ripe for biotechnology that supports agriculture, fisheries and other forms of food production," he says.

Mr. Takenaka enthusiastically encourages founders from all over the world to establish startups in central Japan. "I realize that startups have limited funds. If, however, by reading *Startup Guide Nagoya*, you recognize an opportunity to collaborate with IBIDEN, we invite you to contact us."

About

Since 1912, IBIDEN has been a pioneer in the fields of power generation, ceramics, electronics and building materials. With proud roots in central Japan, IBIDEN aims to be a leader in the global market while remaining attuned to local voices. IBIDEN is committed to continually developing new products that respond to the needs of the world and welcomes collaboration with startups to achieve that aim.

[Contact]   Email: **takehiro_mizutani@ibiden.com** Telephone: **+81-584-81-7973**

[Links]   Web: **ibiden.co.jp**

"*Failure is a fortune. You can make steady progress while making many small mistakes. Work toward the ultimate goal of overcoming failure and creating something better.*"

Building Customer Relationships through Digital Platforms That Exceed Expectations

Masahiro Abe / Senior Executive Manager, Tokai Regional Headquarters at Nippon Telegraph and Telephone West

[Sector] Telecommunications, ICT

A successful platform must simultaneously create value as an intermediary and for the businesses and customers that it connects. "Platforms need to operate in good faith and provide users with peace of mind. Of course, they need to generate profits, but they also need to become a win-win-win situation for all involved," says Masahiro Abe, Nippon Telegraph and Telephone West (NTT-West) senior executive manager of the Tokai Regional Headquarters (covering Aichi, Gifu, Mie and Shizuoka prefectures). A telecommunications industry veteran, Masahiro joined NTT in 1990, and since the mid-2000s he has been focusing his efforts on developing new digital content distribution services such as ebook platforms. Now in charge of NTT-West business in Japan's Tokai region, Masahiro is committed to leveraging ICT to solve problems and enrich the lives of countless customers who depend on the vast NTT-West communications network.

NTT-West is the regional arm of the NTT-Group, Japan's dominant telecommunications company and one of the largest telecommunications companies in the world. However, over the years, the NTT-Group has evolved to provide a variety of products and services. "Our business is more than just providing telecommunications networks," says Masahiro. "We solve customer problems head-on while using the entire spectrum of ICT."

Masahiro has a passion for providing the right platforms to the right customers and has plenty of advice for startup founders seeking to do the same. "When deciding on a target market for your platform, it's important to determine what kind of impact you want to have on society," he says. "Solidify your thoughts on this with your management team. After that, markets and technologies will emerge, and you can decide how they fit with your company."

Masahiro believes that startups can leverage ICT to build better relationships with customers by delighting them with new and unexpected experiences. "In order to build a deeper relationship with customers, it's important to give them a new level of awareness. If you can do this continuously, you'll establish trust," he says. "Startups need to offer something that goes beyond simply meeting the needs of their customers."

Most important tips for startups:

- **Determine your identity.** When establishing a startup, the first thing you need to do is determine what kind of impact you want to make on society.

- **Exceed customer expectations and imagine how they might use your platform.** Do this consistently, and you'll establish trust with your customers.

- **Create a one-of-a-kind product or service.** If your product or service is truly unique, then it will be easier to form alliances with larger corporations.

- **Make use of support programs and organizations.** Regional governments often create programs to support the startup ecosystem. Don't hesitate to take advantage of these programs.

When building an ICT platform that exceeds customer expectations, Masahiro emphasizes the importance of imagination. "When creating a platform, you have to imagine how your customers might use it," he says. "Then, you have to offer your customers peace of mind by being transparent about pricing, communicating value and ensuring that your platform is easy to use."

Masahiro envisions NTT-West as a hub that can connect startups and large firms – something he admits would be difficult for startup founders to do on their own. "NTT-West is a company that is closely linked to the communities it serves. One of the reasons for this is that we are in the community-based infrastructure business. This means that we are involved with all kinds of companies, large and small," he says. However, connecting with large companies requires more than just an introduction. "To make successful connections, a venture should be one of a kind. If your company is truly unique, then it will be much easier to create alliances or connect with corporate clients." According to Masahiro, founders who are interested in starting a business in central Japan should learn the characteristics of the area. "Learn what kind of future the people are envisioning, synchronize with their worldview and unite with their ambitions," he says.

Masahiro eagerly encourages startup founders to contribute to central Japan. "The government has certified Aichi Prefecture, Nagoya city and Hamamatsu city as global hubs, each known as a Global Startup City. There is a lot of support behind this initiative and I want founders to make use of that support," he says. Additionally, organizations such as the Central Japan Economic Federation and the Nagoya Chamber of Commerce have announced support for startups. Lastly, NTT-West created LINKSPARK, a cocreation space where large companies and startups can collaborate in the fields of data science, digital technology and AI.

Ultimately, Masahiro emphasizes the role identity plays in the success of startups. He believes that this will help founders survive the inevitable difficulties that startups face. "Run your business without forgetting the thoughts you had when you first defined your identity. If you embrace trial and error, you will eventually discover a one-of-a-kind product or service."

About

NTT-West is a regional branch of the NTT-Group, Japan's dominant telecommunications company and one of the largest telecommunications companies in the world. NTT-West specializes in providing highly secure, reliable and stable communication networks in the western areas of Japan. Additionally, NTT-West is known for developing ICT solutions and forming strong local ties with the communities it serves.

[Contact] Email: **ddb-reception-nagoya@west.ntt.co.jp** Telephone: **+81-52-291-3829**

[Links] Web: **ntt-west.co.jp** Facebook: **NTTwest** Twitter: **@NTTWestOfficial**

If you embrace trial and error, you will eventually discover a one-of-a-kind product or service.

The Velocity
of Collaboration

Koichi Noguchi / Partner, Global Innovation Factory
at PwC Japan Group

[Sector]   **Assurance, tax, deal advisory, consulting, legal**

For Koichi Noguchi, who leads PwC Japan's Global Innovation Factory, the path
toward new business success depends on startups and corporates fostering
meaningful, collaborative partnerships. With the advent of the digital age, large
companies are trying to keep up with dramatic changes in the business world but
also struggling to transform to meet the needs of their clients. "We need to transform
ourselves and our organizations," says Koichi. "Otherwise, we cannot be successful
in terms of new business and selling new services." Closely working with startups
and adapting to speed, technological innovations, business models and disruptive
ideas are vital to this transformation.

In response to the developing needs of clients and customers, PwC launched
the global initiative PwC Global New Ventures. The initiative, officially launched
in July 2016, works with startups to accelerate their development to leverage
their technology for the corporate and opens up sales and network channels
for these startups.

Koichi leads GIF, a consulting team within PwC Japan Group responsible for startup
partnerships. With his team, Koichi builds powerful partnerships between PwC and
startups that have developed great tech products. "We can support startups by
bringing their product into the market and help them gain visibility as quickly as
possible," he says. "Collaboration brings startups into the light."

One complication to forging powerful partnerships, however, is that as a large-scale
corporate, PwC has tough internal regulations, which makes leveraging partnerships
with startups difficult. "This is a big barrier to overcome," says Koichi. One way GIF
tackles this issue is by having team members dedicated to learning as much as they
can about each of PwC's business units and creating strong collaborative bonds
so that when startups do come in, they integrate well.

On top of this, there's the challenge of relative work styles. "I've learned that one
of the biggest gaps between startups and major companies is speed," says Koichi.
Startups and corporates vary greatly in how quickly they make and adapt to
decisions and changes, as corporates often have deeply rooted internal regulations,
and startups are still finding their regulatory footing.

Most important tips for startups:

- **Be mindful of your pace.** Startups and corporates move at very different speeds. As an entrepreneur, be mindful of the slower pace and stricter regulatory framework of your corporate partners, and adapt to that speed as best as possible. Also, be sure to help your corporate peers adapt to the agility of a startup.

- **Be ready to use your second idea.** In working with a corporate, you should be flexible in your ideas, products and technologies. The second idea found via the partnership may be far stronger for solving the problem you're tackling than the first idea, so you want to be able to adopt this new concept swiftly.

- **Innovate toward social impact.** To partner up with PwC New Ventures, you have to be working toward societal impact and positive change. Your products and technology should solve a real need in the market. This is a vital prerequisite for any startup (local or international) that wants to share their business with PwC in Japan.

In Koichi's opinion, major corporates and startups should find ways to adapt to each other's speeds. Larger companies should catch up with startups in terms of overall pace when they can, and startups should keep in mind that corporates take more time, both strategically and operationally. Koichi believes that when it comes to these kinds of changes, corporates share the responsibility with startups. To foster excellent collaborations between PwC and startups, Koichi and company work toward having an equal, win-win relationship with the startups they partner up with.

Koichi believes that any new startup, whether it's hoping to collaborate with GIF or not, should innovate toward purpose and impact. "New businesses need to be useful in terms of addressing social issues, especially in Japan," he says. Specifically, if you want to collaborate as a startup with Koichi and GIF, you must be working to tackle a societal challenge.

He also advises startups to be able to clearly define the benefits and advantages of future collaborations with every stakeholder and collaborator. This is crucial when working with major companies and academic institutions. "In many cases, the benefits are not clearly defined enough," he says. Be sure to define the benefits at the start of the collaboration and know that they may change during the lifetime of your work together.

It's also important to know that you don't always have to stick with your original idea. "In my experience, the second good idea we come up with through collaborations can be commercialized earlier than the first idea," he says. To get the best products and technologies out of your collaborative efforts, you should be flexible with your ideas.

Finally, Koichi urges startups to attend events hosted by PwC, as the company brings together organizations and initiatives from all over the world to network, pitch to one another and learn from each other's processes. "We host and sponsor various events so me and my team and all the startups have opportunities to interface with stakeholders from across the world," he says. With Koichi at the helm, PwC is poised to learn a lot from its startup partners, so it's recommended that you introduce yourself and your innovations to a corporate that is committed to changing positively with the times.

About

PwC Global New Ventures is PwC's internal SaaS incubator, which collaborates with leading tech companies worldwide to build software solutions that integrate into their existing systems, unlocking business value in real time. PwC Japan's Global Innovation Factory (GIF) team, in collaboration with PwC Global New Ventures, offers a digital platform that leverages partnerships with startups, universities, research institutions and nonprofit organizations from all over the world.

[Contact] Email: **koichi.k.noguchi@pwc.com**

[Links] Web: **pwc.com/jp/en**
pwc.com/gx/en/services/new-ventures.html

"We need to transform ourselves and our organizations; otherwise, we cannot be successful in terms of new business and selling new services."

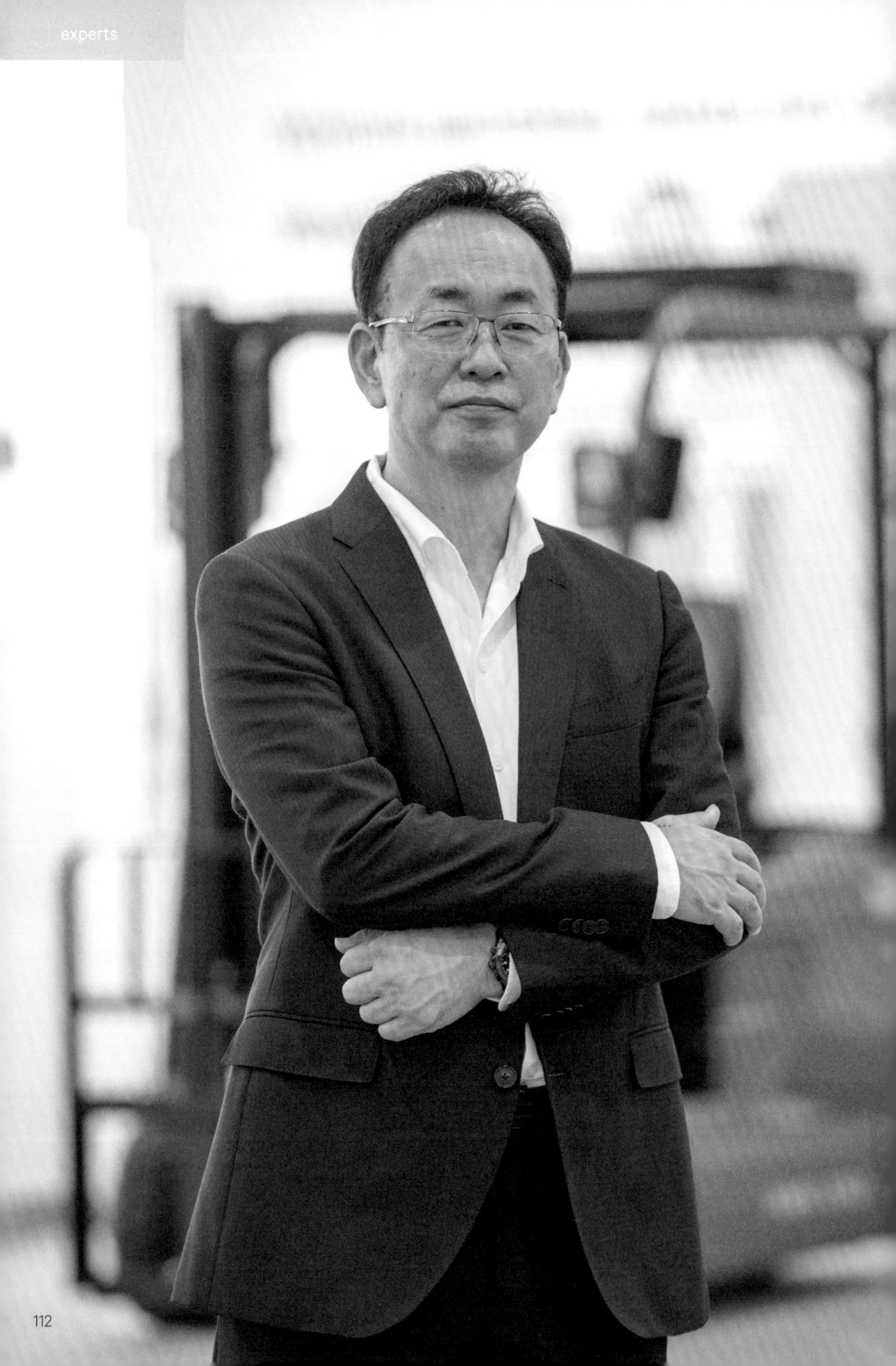

Partnering with Established Corporations to Bring Innovative Ideas to Life

Hisashi Ichijo / Executive Officer and General Manager of R&D Center at Toyota Industries

[Sector] **Textile machinery, materials handling equipment, automobiles and automobile parts**

Toyota Group is the ultimate startup success story. In 1926, Sakichi Toyoda, a serial inventor and entrepreneur, established Toyoda Automatic Loom Works to manufacture and market the looms he had been inventing since the 1880s. In the spirit of "ceaseless innovation," the company rapidly expanded its product line, including the automobile department that was spun off in 1937 to become the world-famous Toyota Motor. Toyoda Automatic Loom Works, now known as Toyota Industries, continues to innovate and expand, leveraging cutting-edge technology to create advanced equipment and vehicles that power complex logistics networks all over the world.

"Our corporate creed, 'Always be studious and creative, striving to stay ahead of the times,' remains in the DNA of the Toyota Group. Since its founding, the Toyota Group has produced multiple generations of innovators creating new products, services and businesses," says Hisashi Ichijo, Toyota Industries executive officer and general manager of R&D Center. Hisashi exemplifies this tradition. As a child, he dreamed of becoming a NASA scientist. He was inspired by the powered suits of the *Gundam* animated series and futuristic technology featured in movies like *Star Wars* and *Star Trek*. "I grew up with the positive notion that technology could solve the various problems facing humanity," says Hisashi. This belief led him to study vehicle robotics at Hokkaido University. Hisashi joined the Industrial Vehicle Division of Toyota Industries in 1987, where he has been responsible for developing advanced technologies for logistics automation ever since. In 2011, he worked with an internal startup to launch a business related to hybrid electronic systems.

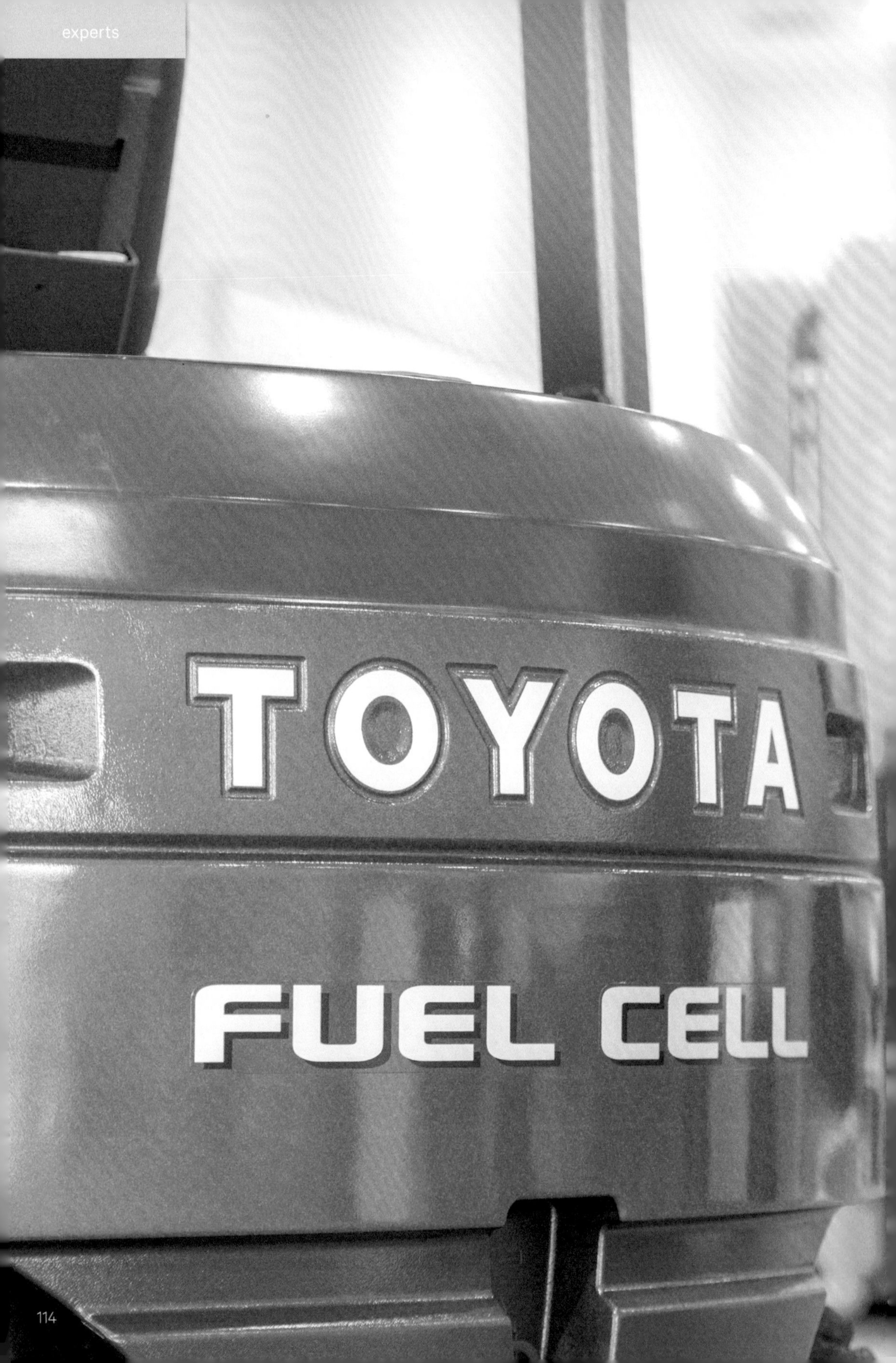
TOYOTA
FUEL CELL

Most important tips for startups:

- **There are opportunities in artificial intelligence and digital transformation.** Manufacturing companies are urgently attempting to digitize their organizations and are looking for support.

- **Explore ways to collaborate with large, established companies.** These companies have the networks and experience to help founders turn their ideas into businesses that can solve social problems.

- **Japan's startup ecosystem has evolved.** Entrepreneurship has become a viable career path and more support is available for startups than ever before.

- **Embrace passion and curiosity.** Founders need to be passionate about their own ideas and technology while being curious about all genres of business.

When it comes to startups that are involved in advanced research and industrialization, Hisashi offers a wealth of advice. "Global leaders in the manufacturing of automobiles, aircraft, machine tools, precision equipment and more are concentrated in the Nagoya area," he says. These companies are eager to leverage new technology such as artificial intelligence and engage in digital transformation. They are actively working on open innovation projects to accomplish this. "This creates numerous opportunities for partnerships with startups," says Hisashi. "Since so many of these companies began as startups, they have a deep understanding of what it takes to launch a new business."

Startup founders often have unrivaled passion for their technology and ideas but lack connections to develop their concepts. Large, established companies are more likely to have the networks and experience to turn these ideas into businesses. "Large companies are also trying to move forward with a sense of urgency," says Hisashi. "If they can empathize with startups, they can grow together." However, large companies can be slow to make decisions and resist the adoption of new technology. "This is akin to a human being's immune response," Hisashi says. "This is an obstacle for startups working with large companies and something I'm trying to resolve."

Even startups based on brilliant ideas and top-notch technology often struggle to gain a foothold in the market. Fortunately, Toyota Industries is working hard to be the partner of choice for entrepreneurs who are eager to call central Japan home. "Startups need partners to work with and accelerators to turn ideas into actual businesses. We aim to address those challenges by acting as an incubator, an accelerator and a mentor," says Hisashi. "We are looking for startups with innovative ideas and cutting edge technologies – even if they are not directly related to our current business domain. If you are interested in our company, please feel free to approach us. Together, let's envision the next century."

Hisashi sees a bright future ahead for those who want to start a business in Japan. "When it comes to startups, Japan had been lagging behind other parts of the world. These days, however, entrepreneurship is now one of the most viable paths for college students," he says. "I believe this is necessary for the future of Japan."

About

Toyota Industries was established in 1926 to produce the automatic looms invented by founder Sakichi Toyoda. A true startup success story, the company has continuously innovated over the last century to become the global leader in three product categories: car air-conditioning compressors, air-jet looms and forklifts.

[Contact]   Email: **startup@mm.toyota-shokki.co.jp**

[Links]   Web: **toyota-industries.com**

" *When bringing new ideas and technology to a large company, it's important to find an open-minded, executive-level decision maker who can be your main point of contact.* "

ders

Takahiro Makino

Founder / Miraiproject

Takahiro Makino graduated from Nagoya University before starting work at Information Services International-Dentsu in Tokyo. After two years, he joined Microsoft and was in charge of their Toyota account before moving to Inspire, a management consultancy and investment fund manager. In 2007, Takahiro returned to Nagoya, where he became the director of IT company Ateam. After Ateam went public in 2012, Takahiro started Miraiproject.

How and why did you start up the company?

In 2010, I was a director of Ateam, a startup based in Nagoya that was preparing to go public. During this busy period, my father was diagnosed with terminal cancer and passed away; you never know when you're going to die. I began to feel a sense of urgency and regretted not being able to take care of my parents, and I started to think about my mother's future care. After Ateam went public, I started my own business to find a way to work that would allow me to spend time with my mother.

What is your business?

We are involved in three businesses. We operate daycare facilities and home nursing-care stations. We also support startups that prioritize contribution to the community over profits and that work with universities. We also invest, with a focus on real estate.

How did you raise money?

I used the capital gains from Ateam's IPO and my experience as finance director at Ateam. I also used my knowledge in dealing with banks to develop my business with bank loans.

What were some of the difficulties you encountered in starting up the business, and how did you solve them?

The nursing and care business inevitably does not yield a profit, and we wanted to provide as much help as possible to startups for free. As we were considering building a new nursing home, we became familiar with real estate and got support from our bank. We started investing in real estate and created a system that allowed us to generate profits to support our endeavors. We have been able to expand our business in both the nursing care field and startup support, and don't have to worry about profits.

What are your company's strengths?

I rely on my experience as a management consultant, investment fund manager and financial officer in a publicly listed company. The bank's support enabled us to get our investment business off the ground. The strength of our investments has allowed us to maintain nursing care and the startup support business, aiming to contribute to the local community. Our strength is integrating all three. We have been able to contribute to the local community of Nagoya by balancing all of our businesses.

What is the best business decision you have ever made?

What I learned during my time at Ateam was that concentrating on a single business was dangerous. In Miraiproject, we managed to avoid the worst of the COVID-19 crisis because we ran multiple businesses. If we had only concentrated on one company, something big might have happened to shake up the entire industry. By having multiple axes of business, we can weather unexpected problems. When I was with Ateam, we started with an official cell phone website. At the time, many companies offered ringtone services, but all of them went out of business. This happened because anyone could make a ringtone, so anyone had a chance. But the record companies and artists held the master recording rights, so you couldn't distribute it without the rights holder's permission. In the era of polyphonic ringtones, the Japanese Society for Rights of Authors, Composers and Publishers would receive the rights fee, but the record companies didn't benefit. From the record companies' point of view, ringtones were the worst business. The moment technological innovation made it possible to distribute ringtones on mobile phones, they jumped into ringtones. The record companies wouldn't give permission to the companies that initially did ringtones. That's when the players changed at once.

My point is that just because a business is growing now, you can't let your guard down. We didn't know how long the official mobile phone website would be profitable, so we decided to start a new business. The company diversified into other activities that used the know-how it had accumulated through its mobile phone website. When Ateam went public, smartphone games were growing, but smartphone games have struggled in the past few years. The companies doing just one smartphone game have fallen into the red, but Ateam is holding on because they have other businesses.

"*I think that you should not trust what investors tell you. For a company to continue to exist for a hundred years, it must have multiple revenue streams.*"

The financial industry tries to make you focus on one area of growth potential. The reason for this is that investors finance a variety of companies and ultimately concentrate on the ones with the highest growth potential. As a result, they hope that a percentage of the total number of companies will be successful. That's why they tell you to select and concentrate on one thing that is likely to grow. But from the management's point of view, they want to start multiple businesses because they don't know what kind of tectonic change is coming, and they have to survive no matter what. From an investor's point of view, it's sometimes better to have you go into the red because they prepare for a stock variation. That is why I think that you should not trust what investors tell you. For a company to continue to exist for a hundred years, it must have multiple revenue streams. I run Miraiproject with this in mind.

What are some of your company's breakthroughs?

Compared to the rapidly changing and evolving IT industry, the rental-condominium-management industry is the most lucrative one for us. I realize that the real estate industry is still very analog. However, we have created a system that can generate profits by thoroughly analyzing and optimizing rent, housing facilities, location and other factors.

We have succeeded in the nursing-care business by making bold investments beyond the industry norm and building a successful daycare facility. Despite the shortage of human resources in the nursing-care industry, we have attracted excellent employees, and the number of users is steadily increasing. As a result, we could keep our recruiting and operating costs considerably lower than our competitors. We have been able to achieve the business results we had anticipated. Operations are running more smoothly than planned.

What is the appeal of the Nagoya area?

Geographically, Nagoya is located in the center of the country and is the only place in Japan where you will soon be able to travel to Tokyo and Osaka in less than an hour after the opening of the linear railway line. Rent is low in Nagoya, and it is a moderately sized city that is an easy place to live. The city is also home to Nagoya University and Nagoya Institute of Technology, both of which have won many Nobel Prizes for their cutting-edge research. The city is a manufacturing-industry center that most notably includes the Toyota Group. As a result, it attracts excellent students and workers from all over Japan.

What are the advantages of starting a business in the Nagoya area?

The stable management and favorable conditions of large companies, mainly from the Toyota Group, make Nagoya an attractive place to start a business. Students in the area are attracted to large companies. Compared to Tokyo, the number of startups is still small. It is easy to receive support from financial institutions and various people involved in the manufacturing sector. Also, there are many factories and warehouses in the surrounding area, making it Japan's best environment for hardware and manufacturing-related startups. Because it is easy to travel to Tokyo on a day trip, you can set up an office in Nagoya, where rent is cheap, and start a business that utilizes the internet while traveling to Tokyo as needed. For this reason, it is possible to start a business at a relatively low cost.

What excites you about the future?

When I was at Microsoft, the exuberance of the internet was extraordinary. It was amazing when I was able to access the official cell phone website on my phone. I think many things will change in the future, probably because of COVID-19, but I believe self-driving will change the world – I think it will take away the time it takes to travel. I spoke at an event sponsored by the Ministry of Land, Infrastructure, Transport and Tourism. I said that the time would come when you will be drinking in Sakae, and a hotel with an automated car will come to the front of the restaurant, you will check-in, work and sleep in the moving vehicle, and then arrive in the morning to visit Tokyo. I think the house and hotel will all be in the car.

[About] Miraiproject aims to build a sustainable business model and contribute to Nagoya and Japan's local community by focusing on socially oriented nursing care and startup support, as well as investing with an emphasis on business profitability.

[Links] Web: miraiproject.co.jp

What are your top work essentials?
Linking the company's goals with personal growth goals.

At what age did you found your company?
Forty-four.

What are your most used apps?
Facebook Messenger and Slack, and of course email.

**What is the most valuable piece of advice
you have been given?**
There was a book published a long time ago by Makoto
Naruke called *Be an Unpopular Adult*. It resonated with
me that you don't have to be able to read the situation
too much.

What is your greatest skill?
I guess I'm good at adapting to the environment.
I've had jobs that I've chosen to do by chance,
but I've loved every job I've had.

Yousuke Okada

Founder and CEO / ABEJA

Nagoya native Yousuke Okada began programming at the age of ten. He studied computer graphics in high school, winning the Minister of Education, Culture, Sports, Science, and Technology Award at the National High School Design Competition. While a college student, he presented his computer-graphics-related research at several international conferences. Yousuke then went on to work for an IT venture and spent time in Silicon Valley, where he witnessed the evolution of artificial intelligence (AI), particularly deep learning. After returning to Japan in 2012, he founded ABEJA, the first startup in Japan to specialize in deep learning. In 2017, he helped found Japan Deep Learning Association, which aims to improve Japan's industrial competitiveness through technology centered on deep learning.

Tell us about your company.
ABEJA provides the ABEJA Platform, an AI-development and -operations platform. The ABEJA Platform delivers a one-stop shop for collecting, labeling, learning, deploying and operating industry-specific data that companies use to focus on developing algorithms tailored to their business. We also offer ABEJA Insight for Retail, an SaaS service based on the ABEJA Platform and specializing in the retail distribution industry.

How did you raise funds?
Our funding was raised primarily via equity financing. Including seed rounds up to Series C, the company has raised over ¥6 billion. ABEJA is the only Japanese company that has received investment from [American multinational technology company] NVIDIA. We're notable for the interest we've received from IT tech giants. We also have investors from Japan's renowned manufacturing companies such as Daikin Industries, Musashi Seimitsu Industry and Topcon. We have the support of both digital companies and nondigital companies. I think both sides expect us to apply digital technology to nondigital businesses and, conversely, to apply nondigital companies' technology to digital companies. I believe this is a significant factor in our ability to raise funds.

What were some of the difficulties and challenges you faced when you started, and how did you solve them?

When we founded the company in 2012, there was little awareness of AI and deep learning, and because of this we had a hard time selling our service. By developing a retail-industry-specific SaaS, it made it easier for companies to understand the benefits of AI. By creating use cases with leading companies across industries, I think we've succeeded in spreading awareness little by little. We also held a large conference called ABEJA SIX, in both 2018 and 2019, and have shared AI implementation and operational examples with the world.

What is your biggest failure to date?

I think I've mostly failed. I know that the word "failure" does not exist in that context, but I see failure as a step that leads to success.

Was there a turning point in your career?

Between the gap that separates ideals from reality, there was a time when I didn't know what to believe in. I think my turning point came when I realized that the decisions I ultimately made, based on my strong initial convictions and intuition, yielded the best results. I decided to embrace that feeling.

What are the strengths of your company?

Developing software that uses AI technology requires a more significant amount of unique know-how than that of traditional software development. ABEJA was one of the first to work on AI since the dawn of deep learning in 2012, and because we have provided AI implementation examples to about two hundred and seventy clients, we have the industry's best know-how.

How do you differentiate yourself from other companies?

By developing multiple businesses, such as an industry-specific SaaS and consulting services, we are able to support every company's AI strategy planning, AI implementation and operations.

Is there anything you wish you had known before you started your business, or anything you feel you should have done differently?

Meeting key people in business is pivotal to leveraging your business. I believe that such people are particularly important in Japan because of its village-society mentality. The essence of sales is the asymmetry of information. Value lies not only in information that everyone knows, but also in the knowledge that comes from that one key individual who has not yet gained attention.

" I think entrepreneurs are destined to suffer forever, and we need to understand this before we dive into it. "

What was the most poignant piece of advice you have received?

The advice I received two years ago from Koji Bando of NTT Plala: "Encounters are the biggest leverage point." In particular, startups tend to fall into a product-oriented mindset, thinking that if you make a good product, people will buy it. But as Peter Thiel says, "If you have performed well in sales, you can dominate the market." Mr. Bando's words allowed me to look at the inconvenient truth from a young company's perspective that no matter how great the product is, it is not enough to capture the market. You have to know how to sell.

When do you find your work most rewarding?

When I feel that I can provide value that will impact the management of our customers.

How do you make use of the opinions of your customers and business partners in your management?

Based on the premise that customers themselves do not realize what they really want, we try not to put too much emphasis on the results of customer interviews. It is important for me to take a bird's-eye view of the client's management philosophy and business processes and develop a hypothesis that the client has not yet realized. I also pay close attention to how customers react when I propose a hypothesis to them.

What issues are you currently facing?

The world has changed due to the spread of the new coronavirus infection, so I think we need to think about how we should change.

What are your goals and outlook for the future?

To become a company that is indispensable to society. We want to create a situation where the business processes of many companies are on the ABEJA Platform.

What are some of the exciting innovations in the deep learning industry?

The deep learning industry is changing at a fantastic pace. In October 2012, Dr. Jeffrey Hinton of the University of Toronto showed off deep learning's incredible possibilities. Initially, one of the breakthroughs was the use of deep learning in areas such as computer vision and image recognition. Around October 2018, the area of natural language processing showed significant advancement.

What professional advice would you give to those who are currently thinking of starting a business or just starting one?

If someone is on the fence about an enterprise, I would say, "Why not try it first?" The gap between ideals and reality is suffering caused by entrepreneurship. However, I also believe that you should quit the company the moment you stop suffering; this is because if the gap between your ideals no longer causes suffering, it means that there is no room for the company to grow. So I think entrepreneurs are destined to suffer forever, and we need to understand this before we dive into it.

What is the appeal of working in the Nagoya area?

Toyota and the many companies that were influenced by Toyota create opportunities. In a sense, I think Toyota is pretty crazy because it was founded when we lost the war, and yet it was able to see a way to take over the US car industry and became a global standard. Nagoya is an exciting area to try to build the next generation of the automotive industry.

When I think of Nagoya, I think of the mindset "It is all about the local area." Many companies stick to this without adapting technology to other areas. Conversely, Toyota is a company that has become a global standard because of its Galapagosization (the Galapagos syndrome), basically pursuing its own style. For example, the Japanese mobile phone business did not do well, but I believe this was due to the fact that they did too much market research on what Japan wanted. I think that we should continue to promote Japan's Galapagosization. We should have our own style and promote it.

There are both positive and negative aspects of Galapagosization. On the one hand, it is a good thing that the Galapagos system has given rise to Toyota's production methods of improving their products. On the other hand, when it is pushed to the limit, it becomes a highly specialized system with no versatility. I think this will come and go in waves. Japan has pushed manufacturing to the limit. The accumulation of these efforts has led to the present-day situation in which Japan is dominant in the improvement process and building up operation.

I firmly believe that when it comes to business, it's better to catch the second wave. If we break out of the current process, we can introduce a new system that will increase fifty to a hundred times and make good use of it and overtake the US system. I think we will be able to bring back the era when Japan is number one again, and I believe this will involve the area of deep learning.

[About]   ABEJA maintains a platform that acquires industry-specific data and develops specialized algorithms for companies. It also provides ABEJA Insight for Retail, an SaaS service tailored to the retail distribution, manufacturing and infrastructure industries.

[Links]   Web: abejainc.com LinkedIn: company/abeja-inc. Facebook: abejainc Twitter: @ABEJA_Inc

What are your top work essentials?
It's important to do things differently. In terms of
company strategy, I think it is important to keep going
in the opposite direction from the current trends.

At what age did you found your company?
Twenty-three.

What are your most used apps?
Slack.

**What is the most valuable piece of advice
you've been given?**
Encounters are the biggest leverage point.

What is your greatest skill?
Saying something I don't understand in order
to evoke differing opinions.

Yuichiro Iwaki

Founder and Representative Director / SPEED

Originally from Seto, Yuichiro Iwaki founded SPEED in 2012. In school, Yuichiro didn't feel he was particularly good at anything other than music because he never received much positive feedback. However, once he started working in restaurants and selling computers, he received compliments on his work and sales ability. It was then that he realized that he was better suited to the business world, where he could not only sell but also create.

What was your entrepreneurial path?

It began when I participated in a digital-content promotion event in Nagoya. That's when I realized that to sell products, you need to do many things. I started to think that maybe I was a salesman. But I didn't think simply being a salesman was very cool. When I was younger, I would clash with my friends when we had different approaches, even though we had the same goal. In my thirties, I started to put myself in other people's shoes. Then I thought, "putting myself in another person's shoes is a business." So when I started making games, animation and movies, I thought it was essential to think about how much fun the audience would have by putting myself in their shoes.

I have always loved images. When I was in elementary school, I wanted to be a cartoonist. I was an early believer that the digital revolution would dramatically alter all aspects of entertainment, culture and how we live. In the last five years, I feel that the rapid pace of technological innovation has allowed me to accomplish things I saw coming twenty years ago. I initially thought that creating and managing were two different things, so I stopped making things to focus on management. I've come to believe that's not right. In the end, I was just a manager. Some people who create things have to single-task to immerse themselves in their work positively. I'm a multitasker. I look at things from multiple angles. I ended up on the management side because, especially in our industry, many people just want to create. I started to be in charge of money and contracts, and I began to understand agreements. I wasn't aware that we don't like to talk about money and contracts very much in Japan, but I thought I might be good at it.

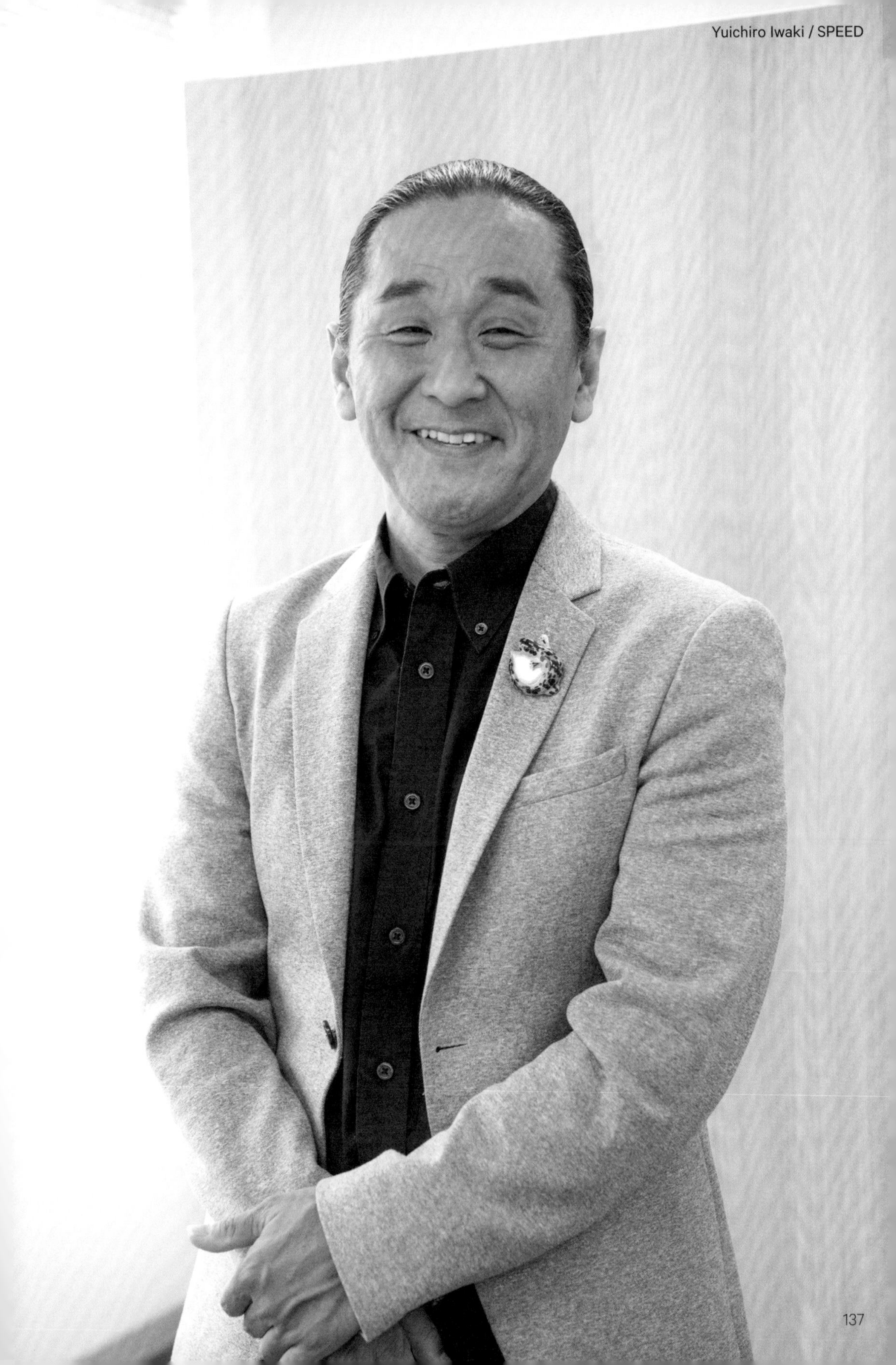

As my role became more management oriented, I had more opportunities to meet with people from various companies. I was planning for both the mass market and the core market. While I also worked on films that most people would see, the core fans were in a high value-added, high-revenue structure. At the time, just before the internet and social networking sites came out, I thought it would be a core market in the future. I thought the mass market would remain, of course, but the masses will get out of the way, and that's where the core market will be pivotal.

What was it like when you first started your company?

Having a company is like raising a child. It's hard work. But it's harder if you're not careful; it's a 365-days-a-year gig. It's hard if you think it's hard. I wouldn't say it's a lot of fun, though. In the beginning, the people in the government were very supportive, as was my tax accountant. We had the support of experts in various fields, so there were no particular difficulties. In Japanese, we say, "A rice-cake maker is a rice-cake maker." It's a metaphor meaning that it's best to leave everything to the experts. It's also a metaphor for the fact that even if you're good at something and are still an amateur, you're not as good as an expert.

Is there anything you wish you had known before starting the company?

Not particularly. And the less you know, the better. You always have to learn before you start, but you can learn too much. It's all about action. While you're running, reality is happening side by side with you. You have to take the time to watch and observe. You have to make sure you're awake after you've begun. It's more like a review than a prep. You have to take it easy and yet take it seriously as well. The more you know, the more risk you take and the more cramped you feel. If it's just information you are after, it's obtainable.

For some reason, everyone looks at the beginning and the end. But the big picture is essential. Even if you are thinking about what you are going to eat today, you don't think about what you will do in ten years. Even when I create a character in computer graphics, I don't start with the details. First of all, I make a form out of clay. That's how we did it in school. Knowledge tends to come later, so in that sense, it's better not to know in advance. You can think about it later on as a bad idea.

"*Putting myself in another person's shoes is a business.*"

What's the best decision you've made since you started the company?

Starting the company was the best decision I've ever made. We started out in Seto. I left it to the professionals to do what I should let them do. I didn't even look at the properties in Seto. The professionals I chose to assist me were trustworthy people. It took more courage to leave the decisions up to them. Sure it's safer to do it myself no matter what happens, but if I did that, why would I hire them?

Eventually, I will bite the bullet on who I work with; I trust them from the beginning. I don't look at careers or backgrounds; I only look at how they are as people. Age doesn't matter either. Sometimes the people we're interacting with in our business right now are twenty-something kids. They're closer to digital natives than I am, and their ideas are different. In some ways, they are more skilled than me. There are times when I don't understand what the younger kids are saying, but that's a good thing. If you don't believe in them, they won't develop. If I do everything to suit my tastes, I'll end up with a Shōwa-era Japanese flavor. I am confident in my ability to run my business. But it's not just about confidence in myself, it's about how to involve the people around me.

Do you have any advice for people starting a business?

There was a novel and movie called *Saga's Grandma Gabai*. Grandma Gabai said not to think about hard things in the middle of the night. She said, "Don't think about it after 2 AM. Go to bed. Think about it in the morning." It's a continuation. To continue, you have to be healthy. When you're not feeling well, your thinking can decline. I don't pack too much in at night. When you start a business, it's going to be hard – cash flow, staff, etc. But you have to solve the problems one by one and make decisions. It's just one thing after another, and it's only a matter of time before you feel better. It's crucial to maintain your energy to keep going.

So the middle of the night is not a good time for me to think. Though I was a night person, it's an environment where you're too focused. There's no other information coming in. If you continue to focus on one thing, you can become confused, so you have to figure out how to mitigate it mentally. I have tried all kinds of things, like going on a trip or going out for a drink, because I was having a hard time at work. People's ability to think is dispersed. You can't come to a suitable solution by focusing on one thing. While you have to keep thinking, you can't overthink it. It's a contradiction. Can you play with that contradiction? Can you go out with your friends or raise your children when you're thinking about such inconsistencies? It requires training.

What's the best thing about working in Nagoya?

Nagoya is compact, even though it's a big city. The people, the place, the connections, everything. I think customers are closer to each other, not so much physically, but more in terms of interaction. The more people you have, the less likely you are to have meaningful encounters. I think it's a matter of density. In areas where there are a lot of companies, people come and go a lot. You can talk to people in Nagoya thanks to the creation of deeper connections. On a personal note, I like Nagoya because I love cars. In Tokyo, the trains are tiring.

[About]   SPEED creates digital content in the entertainment, rehabilitation and medical care sectors using 3D computer graphics, VFX, VR, motion graphics and 2D animation. It is also active in the production and planning of music videos, live images and live-action films. The company has studios in Tokyo, Nagoya and Seto.

[Links]   Web: speedinc-jp.com Facebook: SPEEDINC.JP Instagram: speedinc_jp Twitter: @SPEEDINC_JP

What are your top work essentials?
Think in the morning. Don't think about things after 2 AM.
Go to bed.

At what age did you found your company?
Thirty-nine.

What are your most used apps?
Google Meet.

**What is the most valuable piece of advice
you have been given?**
If you want to do it, do it. Move.

What is your greatest skill?
Presentation. All communication is presentation.

Yumiko Tokita

Founder and CEO / CURUCURU

Yumiko Tokita was born in Aichi and received an MBA from GLOBIS University. Initially, she worked as a CTO of IT security. Her childhood dream was to create a company that enriches women's lifestyles. When she founded her company in 2008, she chose to focus on golf because she saw it as a great way to make new friends of all ages and genders. For the past few years, she has been a regular contributor on women's marketing in golf industry magazines.

What was your entrepreneurial path?

I decided to start a business when I was a child. My father passed away when I was four years old, and I suddenly became part of a family of three with my mother and sister. I wondered why my mother was struggling so much and why I had to work so hard, even though I was a child. It felt unreasonable. I thought that a society where someone has to fight alone is wrong. But at the same time, I was also impressed by the relationships that my mother had. I remember that volleyball saved her. I learned that you could overcome difficult circumstances if you have friends. There was a time when friends and others supported me, and I realized that to live life to the fullest, I had to help my friends. I want to create a world where people don't feel alone, no matter what kind of environment they live in. This has become my life ambition. I wanted to contribute to society by creating a business to achieve this goal. The first time I took on the challenge of starting a business was in my early twenties, and it didn't go well. I started my current company when I was thirty.

What early struggles did you face, and how did you overcome them?

Two things caused me problems. The first was that I had no industry knowledge or connections. For example, when I wanted to start a golf apparel ecommerce business specializing in young women, I didn't know how to manage inventory. Secondly, I didn't have anyone to talk to as an entrepreneur. I had no one with whom to discuss how to expand our user base or solve our management problems. I wasted time and repeated small mistakes, but I was able to sign up for outside coaching and advice, and I learned how to build a network of contacts in Nagoya and Tokyo. This was a positive thing. It helped me get over the hump.

Also, our company's only source of funding was debt financing, so I was careful to be aware of our financial statements and avoided going into the red. I had a safe investment style. I was so focused on increasing revenue and profit that I phased in our system and personnel investments, which led to service growth.

The biggest failure in decision-making I made was allowing the capacity of operations and mechanisms that support service growth to lag behind demand. This was because we gradually made investments in systems and personnel. As a result, we were unable to fulfill our responsibility to our users and business partners.

Were there any turning points in your business?
There were two: one was the tailwind created when golf became a popular movement among young people. Golf used to be a sport for fathers. Now, it has changed and is considered a fashionable lifestyle. The fact that we were in a good position to take advantage of this at that time was very positive. The other factor was a change in our management perspective. The 2011 earthquake and COVID-19 each caused a pinch for our company. We reassessed what the company is for and what our mission is. When you go back to your vision and reaffirm your commitment to accomplish something, you have a clear idea of what you want to do and what needs to be done.

What is your company's strength?
Our wonderful users. Interacting with them makes it possible to update our mindset and make changes before other companies can. I feel that B2C companies have the advantage of having cultures that strive to create user value without wavering, in good times and bad. We operate in niche areas that appeal to women, such as fertility and the golf market. Our user-first attitude of making a difference in their lives makes us a good fit even in the current COVID-19 situation. We will not waver, even in a disaster. We value a sense of trust and are determined to continue meeting the expectations of our users.

How do you differentiate yourself from other companies?
We are a company with a niche differentiation strategy. For example, women golfers make up only ten percent of the golf market. That's where the problems and needs that only women golfers have exist. By solving those specific problems and needs, we can create value that other companies cannot provide. Also, we differentiate ourselves by branding the company as one that meets users' expectations.

"*It's all about articulating your mission and vision.*"

Is there anything you wish you had known before starting your own business?
It is essential not to try to do things all by yourself. Ask for help from others. There are many people outside the company who can help you, help with your dream or whom you can ask for advice. It's a normal thing for me now, but I wish I had done it sooner.

What was the most poignant piece of advice you have received in the past?
Even Ichiro (the famous baseball player) bats thirty percent out of one hundred. Even professionals swing the bat ten times, but only hit it three times or fewer. This is a lesson in the importance of how many times you must swing the bat because the number of failures is naturally higher. If I'm going to fail, I don't want to fail in a small way. I want to be bold, to challenge myself, and fight the good fight even when I fail.

When do you find business most rewarding?
Our services are often based on the theme of problem-solving, so when the value of one of our services is conveyed to us by users, I feel happy that I created it. For example, someone saying "I started playing golf through your site and made a friend for life," or "Thanks to the Fertility Voice social networking service, I was recommended for fertility treatment." This kind of feedback is rewarding.

How do you make use of the feedback from your customers in your business?
We conduct a survey of two thousand users every year and also conduct user interviews. User feedback has two roles. The first is to understand the needs and demands of our users. The other purpose is to understand the issues that users do not yet see or have been unable to articulate. We want to create services that are one step ahead of the competition, so we use this information to improve and develop services.

Are you facing any current issues?
Each business has its own set of challenges, but we are facing several market issues. Our golf fashion business has already captured thirty percent of the young women's ecommerce market, which we have been targeting, so we need to expand our market and respond to our users' diversifying needs. Our fertility-focused social networking business is all about market recognition, but privacy about pregnancy is an issue we have to consider when increasing our presence.

What are your goals and outlook for the future?

We aim to become Japan's leading lifestyle innovation company that creates connections with friends, family and colleagues. To this end, we aim to expand our golf business from women in their twenties and forties to men and other sports. In particular, one of our goals is to create the best sports fashion ecommerce site in Japan.

What professional advice would you give to those who are thinking of starting a business or who have just started their own business?

It's all about articulating your mission and vision. First of all, articulating your mission is a pledge to yourself when you start a business. Then, you will use it to tell someone else about your dream, and it will give you the chance to gather a group of friends with a similar mindset. Businesses exist to realize a mission and a vision, and strategies must be created to align them. You can also turn to your mission and vision in times of hardship, and they can function as a decision-making axis for management when making significant choices.

What is the appeal of working in the Nagoya area?

First is the ease of living in the city. It has affordable rent, nature and it is a good environment for raising children. There are plenty of universities, vocational schools and hospitals. It's a city that has the power to invest in things when it's motivated. Second is the location. It is a major transportation hub. The travel time to Tokyo is short, and it has an international airport and an abundance of hotels. I currently live in Tokyo and commute to Nagoya once a week, but it's an hour and a half one way, so there's no inconvenience.

[About] CURUCURU focuses on two sectors: golf and life events. The Golf Life business promotes the idea that golf can expand your circle of friends. Its popular website includes an ecommerce platform for golf clothing, a free club rental service, articles and a platform to search for like-minded friends. The Life Event business operates a social networking service for women trying to conceive.

[Links]   Web: curucuru.co.jp Facebook: curucuru.jp Twitter: @curucuru_golf

What are your top work essentials?
Dreaming.

At what age did you found your company?
Thirty.

What are your most used apps?
Chatwork.

**What is the most valuable piece of advice
you have been given?**
You can swing the bat ten times and hit it three
times or fewer, so swing often.

What is your greatest skill?
I am persistent.

Yuriko Kato

Founder and President / M2 Labo

Yuriko Kato is from Chiba and graduated from Tokyo University in 1998. After receiving a master's degree in precision farming from Cranfield University in the UK, she worked at NASA, where she looked at ways to produce food in space. She founded agtech company M2 Labo in 2009, and the company has established itself as an innovator in logistics and distribution.

What was your entrepreneurial path?

I have two children, and I thought about contributing to society as a mother. I didn't want to be a researcher of industrial machines. I didn't plan to be away from my children and my husband. I started out wanting to do a job that would allow me to give more directly back to children. When I was a student, I chose to study agriculture because I was interested in the environment and in food issues. At first, I didn't set out to make a big company. I wanted to do something that would allow me to say to my children, "This was helpful, even if only for a little while." That was when I launched my first company. It wasn't a company that I started with an idea – I didn't have a business model.

What was the best decision you ever made?

We are an agricultural think tank, and we are involved in planning businesses that combine different aspects of agriculture to solve social problems. One of the best decisions I have made was establishing Yasai Bus [meaning "vegetable bus"] based on the fruit and vegetable distribution business. We started four years ago with the hypothesis that it would be a good idea and have been working to improve the distribution system for agricultural products. It's a combination of ecommerce and shared logistics. Initially, it was very expensive to ship using Yamato Transport or other door-to-door delivery services. However, if you're doing this in the local area, transport is not as costly. We could all share a truck, and whoever wanted to use it and run it around the area would benefit because it was cheaper to use. I think the idea of the vegetable bus has stuck with everyone. We are speeding up the pace of development by creating a fair and open system for collaboration. Our win-win business concept has received a certain amount of positive feedback. Additionally, we have added logistics functions to the company. Three years ago, we established a separate company to develop and sell transport robots and IoT systems, which are now in use in agriculture and other fields.

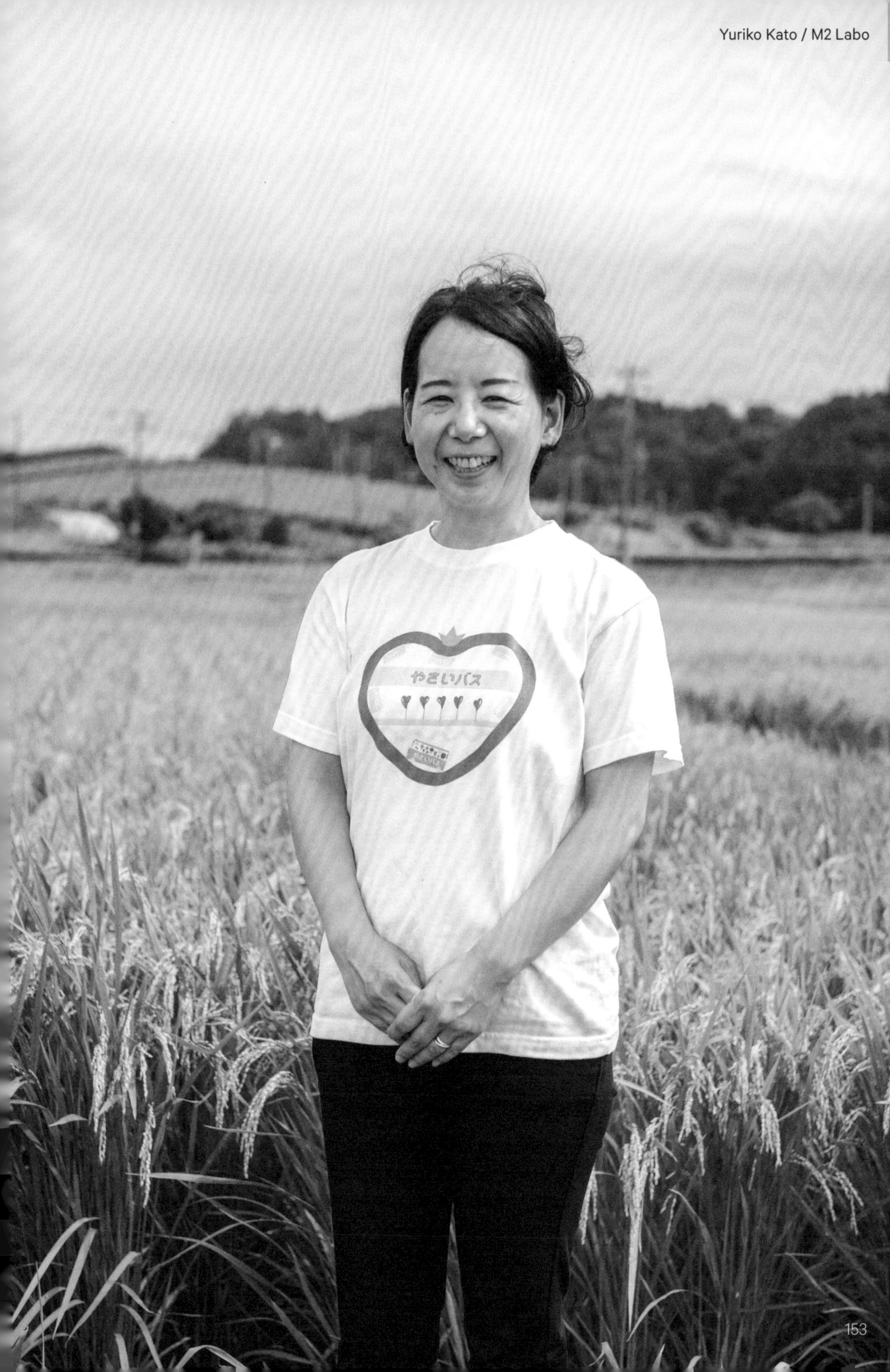
やさいバス

What has been the biggest mistake you have made so far, and how did you overcome it?

Before creating the Yasai Bus business, I had invested in building a fruit and vegetable distribution system. I think I spent about ¥10 million in total. I'm embarrassed to say, but there was a shortage of funds, and so we had to discontinue development. This was my biggest mistake. In the end, we made it smaller and revised it to create a system that matched our sales scale. Later, when the company had its first profitable month, large companies in the region (Suzuyo and Suzuki) invested in it through their subsidiaries. We were able to make a profit. Thanks to their support, we were able to overcome this difficult situation. Our unchanging philosophy and efforts to improve the region's future led to investment from these two companies. Today our experience in designing, building and running our own highly sustainable service allows us to provide qualified guidance and support to clients who come to us for advice.

What's your greatest skill?

Creating a win-win relationship. I know it isn't commonly said, especially in the agriculture business, but I'm good at conceptualizing a business idea where everyone is happy. When I make a business model or business plan I want it to be win-win.

What issues are you currently facing?

We often collaborate with other companies, which makes it challenging to achieve speed, and we would like to improve our project management capabilities.

What have been the turning points in your career?

The first turning point was creating the first women's program accepted by the Development Bank of Japan. We won the grand prize in the business plan competition. In a single moment, we became known not only in Shizuoka Prefecture but across the country.

The second turning point was a significant price increase in logistics, primarily transportation. Even before the considerable price increase in February 2017, logistics costs had been rising. For vegetables, the shipping cost was about ¥1,500 versus ¥1,000 previously. So, since about 2014, we have been researching a joint delivery network in Shizuoka Prefecture, and in the fiscal year 2016, we began experimenting with a joint delivery business with the Shizuoka Prefectural Government. Then there was a sudden price hike, so we decided to continue the experiment as a private sector business, so we founded Yasai Bus.

Thirdly, the COVID-19 situation has increased interest in our food in the community. The Yasai Bus is a distribution service that has given up the last mile; people don't touch the food much and it's fresh. It's a system that arrives in the community and uses IT, so the number of users is increasing.

"*It is essential to be considerate and don't give up. Evolve every day!*"

What are your thoughts on the future of agriculture and the expansion of
your work?

People should give more thought to agriculture. Ideally, it would be a situation where
people would think about the countryside, the community and the effort they're
making, and about what makes it sustainable. Nowadays, you can buy food twenty-
four hours a day at a convenience store, so fundamentally we aren't thinking carefully
about our food. I think this is weakening the agriculture industry in a way that is
very significant. This is an issue that we need to work on permanently. In the case
of Japanese agriculture, we need to protect our local communities and ensure that
we can do so sustainably and organically. I've already decided to expand in Japan
this year, mainly to Hiroshima and other places, and I've already found a partner. So I
think we'll be able to cover most of Japan in the next two to three years. It'll be like a
franchise, just using our base.

We believe that our services are designed to be "glocal" and are adaptable to other
parts of the world. We've already started to prepare for this. We're getting calls from
other places, such as Africa, where they want to do a vegetable bus, and we're going
to be doing a lot of it. If an area in need of food introduces sustainable production
and sustainable consumption, then I think we can get by with 10 billion people on
the planet.

If you could do it all over again with the knowledge you have now, what would you
do differently?

As I mentioned earlier, M2 Labo started as a company without a business model.
I think I should have discussed the business concept with several people before
starting the business. After all, business creation is often tricky to get through on
your own, so it is vital to have a partner even before you expand your business;
it is a great driving force. Looking back, I should have found more business partners
before I started. I think I would have been better able to run the business. I think
finding a partner was the hardest part.

What professional advice would you give to someone who is currently thinking about starting a business or just starting one?

It's better to have friends. Often you meet them while doing business, but you can share the struggles of starting a business. I think it is more fun to start a business if you have a partner. You should also have the financial resources (more than a year's worth) to support your personal life. The only way to do this is always to have a fast loop of learning, thinking and action. It is essential to be considerate and don't give up. Evolve every day!

What is the best thing about the Nagoya area and its vicinity?

We are good at making things, and this is the only area in the world where you can get everything you need when you want to make something. We are able to manufacture products at a very high level. What makes me happy is the increase in the number of collaborators and customers who understand our business philosophy and are willing to work with us. We have many customers who know that the business we are creating is a business of cocreation and are eager to do business with us, so we worry, think and act together. Additionally, there are many large, stable companies here, especially Toyota, and many young people. They want to do something, so you might be able to pull that energy out of them. It is fascinating!

[About]   M2 Labo is dedicated to solving the logistical and distribution problems of agriculture and is active in the development of transport robots and IoT systems that are viable in other fields. It is focused on creating a sustainable society in Japan by utilizing unique analytical techniques and social business models.

[Links]   Web: m2-labo.jp Facebook: M2labo

What are your top work essentials?
Affection for all aspects of my job.

At what age did you found your company?
Thirty-four.

What are your most used apps?
Google and Slug.

**What is the most valuable piece of advice
you have been given?**
It doesn't matter how small it is, as long as
it's useful to society.

What is your greatest skill?
I'm good at conceptualizing business ideas.

ools

- **Be artistic in your thinking.**
  You should be a free and creative artistic thinker. Be in touch with your art, and train yourself not to lose it.

- **Respect the values of others when making decisions.**
  Successful students are respectful of different values and work well with others.

- **Be both bold and subtle.**
  Be prepared to learn how to cultivate these aspects when working with other artists.

- **Find friends with different ideas.**
  We are looking for students who are open to new ideas and viewpoints. You won't be developing your talents on your own and should seek diversity in your company, art and creations.

[Name]
Aichi University of the Arts

[Elevator Pitch]
"We are one of the few public universities in Japan dedicated to music and the arts. Our university is committed to the development and dissemination of art and culture."

[Enrollment]
Students per year: 1,000

[Description]
Aichi University of the Arts was founded in 1966 for the purpose of creating a cultural sphere in the central Japan region. As well as undergraduate and graduate programs in fine arts, it offers music programs, art theory courses and has an institute for the conservation of cultural property. Its international exchange programs with world-renowned universities such as Cologne University of Music and Dance and Silpakorn University encourage students to explore new perspectives and bring foreign influences to the school. In addition, it hosts an artist-in-residence program that invites artists from around Japan and overseas to its campus to collaborate on educational, performance and creative activities.

The overall mission of Aichi University of the Arts is threefold: to foster excellence in the arts, to be a center for the creation and dissemination of international art and culture and to contribute to the development of art and culture in cooperation with society. It aims to foster a stronger relationship between artists and wider society, and to do this it encourages the use of design thinking and creative and artistic thought to leap towards innovation.

The university is developing a program called the Art Innovation Lab, which aims to strengthen the relationship between the arts and society through art innovation. Its organizers hope to accelerate a two-way value exchange between art and business and encourage problem solving through artistic thought. The program will share seed technology from companies in the Tokai region and research from other universities, and the overall goal is to create opportunities for new breakthroughs and generate new ideas to share with startups. The university currently has projects in which fine art students participate in corporate business development, and the newly established New Media & Image Division will also increase the number of points of contact between art and society through video and media. The university welcomes collaboration with private businesses, companies, and municipalities to further such endeavors.

[Apply to]
aichi-fam-u.ac.jp/english/admission

[Links]
Web: **aichi-fam-u.ac.jp**

- **Be prepared to apply practical business skills.**
  GLOBIS students focus on applying practical business
  skills to realize social transformation through value
  creation in their businesses.

- **Have a positive attitude.**
  We encourage students to have a positive mindset.
  As future leaders, we expect students to be the source
  of positivity and inspiration for others.

- **Seek a life-changing experience.**
  GLOBIS can offer a life-changing experience to those
  who want to contribute towards building a better
  and more innovative society.

- **Be altruistic.**
  If your classmates are in trouble, it is essential to be
  altruistic and try to help them. We expect students
  to support each other in handling the difficulties they
  will face.

[Name]
GLOBIS University

[Elevator Pitch]
"We are dedicated to supporting and producing visionary leaders who create and innovate societies. GLOBIS can offer a life-changing experience for those who are thinking of embarking on their startup journey, contributing to society and bringing about change."

[Enrollment]
Total enrollment: 1,095 (2020)

[Description]
President and founder Yoshito Hori started GLOBIS with a marketing class taught from a small Tokyo apartment in 1992. Since then, the school has committed to producing highly motivated leaders who are willing to challenge business norms and initiate social change. The core GLOBIS educational philosophy is based on three main pillars: practical knowledge and skills, an extensive professional network and a personal mission. In addition to its Nagoya campus, GLOBIS has locations in Tokyo, Osaka, Sendai and Fukuoka. In 2020, it opened a special campus in Yokohama where students can undertake the first half of an MBA before completing the program online. In 2009, the school launched a part-time English MBA program, followed by a full-time version in 2012 and an online one in 2017. With over a thousand people enrolled in the Japanese MBA program each year (both on campus and online), GLOBIS is the largest business school in Japan.

In addition to its MBA programs, GLOBIS also provides a pre-MBA program that helps students jump-start their MBA journey by starting with just one course in an area of their interest. In the pre-MBA, students can select classes according to their objectives and availability.

In 2015, GLOBIS devised the concept of "technovate" to develop human resources for innovation through technology, and since then has created more than ten technovate courses. The technovate program is based on the belief that the ability to apply technology to business is important for future business leaders. GLOBIS has developed a curriculum that includes teaching materials based on case studies and informed by venture capital–funded business. In one example, it uses the knowledge of Takram, a design innovation firm that makes it possible for companies and organizations to create new design-driven businesses. Technovate courses aim to teach a new way of thinking about design, and they are taught by industry experts who provide students with the knowledge they need to take advantage of new technologies.

[Apply to]
mba.globis.ac.jp/admissions

[Links]
Web: mba.globis.ac.jp Facebook: Globis.official Instagram: mba_globis Twitter: @GLOBIS_nagoya

- **Be strong, yet kind.**
  In today's society, it is necessary for women to have
  strength: the strength to think for themselves when
  faced with challenges and the strength to use their
  knowledge and skills in society. The kindness to care
  for others and to recognize others is a sign of dignity.

- **Understand how other people feel.**
  Put yourself in other people's shoes and try
  to understand their perspective.

- **Be prepared for different perspectives.**
  It is essential to understand and study everyone's role.
  Applying what you learn will change the way you work
  when you collaborate with others in the workplace,
  and this is important to get your work done.

- **Measure how far you are from your essence.**
  Don't be troubled if you are far from your goals. Being
  aware of how far away you are from them allows you to
  keep thinking about how to achieve them.

[Name]
Kinjo Gakuin University

[Elevator Pitch]
"We are a women's college rooted in the evangelical Christian spirit and are dedicated to sending our graduates out into the world with a rich love of humanity and a deep academic education."

[Enrollment]
Total enrollment: 5,164 (2020)

[Description]
Kinjo Gakuin University began as Kinjo Girl's School in 1889, when it was founded by Presbyterian missionary Annie Randolph, who was concerned about the lack of progress in women's education in Nagoya and felt the need for women to develop character through scripture. By 1949, it was one of the major women's universities in the Tokai region, and today it offers twelve undergraduate departments in five different colleges, as well as graduate programs. In 2020, the school held the title for producing the most female company presidents of any school in Aichi for the sixth year in a row.

The university's philosophy is that it isn't an extension of high school or a link to getting a job. Rather, the curriculum focuses on solving social issues and is founded in the belief that college is a time to experience that failing is a part of learning, even if it occurs multiple times. The university searches for ways to partner with industry and government, with an aim of helping students learn how to solve social problems by responding to societal needs.

The Women's Leadership Initiative (WLI) and the Kinjo International Training (KIT) are two of the university's unique programs. The former develops its students' leadership skills and is focused on collaborative leadership, challenging students to understand their power to build a society where each individual can play an active role. KIT is a study-abroad course that is taken in a student's first year with an aim of expanding their perspective. The university has also established the Women's Mirai Research Center, offering women of all ages diverse learning programs, professional career counseling and exchange events.

[Apply to]
kinjo-u.ac.jp

[Links]
Web: kinjo-u.ac.jp Facebook: kinjo.univ Instagram: kinjogakuin_university

- **Be able to visualize.**
  We are looking for people with the ability to envision.
  Those who aren't able to imagine don't belong
  in manufacturing.

- **Believe in yourself.**
  People who believe in themselves can chase their
  dreams by saying, "Let's create a venture!" They can
  work hard because they can visualize what it will look
  like when they reach their goal.

- **Have a firm grasp of current technology.**
  Know what current technology can do and why it is
  useful. This knowledge will enable you to offer ideas
  and methods to future endeavors and companies.

- **Get people involved.**
  The ability to involve yourself is crucial to the ability
  to include others.

- **Be able to empathize with people.**
  The ability to empathize resonates with others,
  and it opens up a dialogue that allows you to explain
  your ideas.

[Name]

Nagoya Institute of Technology

[Elevator Pitch]

"We focus on imagination and the ability to tell a story about the near future market. We think about what to develop to meet the needs of that market."

[Enrollment]

Total enrollment: 5,771 (2020)

[Description]

Nagoya Institute of Technology, also known as NITech, was founded in 1905 as the Nagoya Higher Technical School with the purpose of developing the industries of the central Japan region and encouraging the pursuit of careers in industry. Situated in Japan's industrial heartland, the school prides itself on being one of the region's leading engineering institutes, offering both undergraduate and graduate programs in a range of engineering fields and producing creative and independent thinkers who embrace new industries and technologies. It has a mission to develop revolutionary science and technologies, fostering rich human resources and contributing to the peace and social welfare of the future by consistently producing and developing new industries and culture. The school has several educational research centers, including the Research Center for Nano Devices and Advanced Materials and NITech AI Research Center.

NITech focuses on the importance of monetization in companies, subscribing to the idea that the faster you build and develop, the quicker you can enter the market to recoup your investment. The importance of timing to market is inherent in the education that students receive. The Management of Technology (MOT) master's program, which attracts working professionals, entrepreneurs and researchers, is particularly focused on market preparation. Students enter with a research theme in mind and develop it using the MOT concept, which is based on education and research on market value creation backed by technology. Students learn the methodology of ascribing value to technology with an eye toward the future. The program aims to help students develop business plans for their companies or startups and teaches students how to formulate and implement regional industrial technology policies.

The school also offers a technical management class on backcasting – the concept of determining steps to achieve an outcome by working back from the desired objective. Undergraduate and graduate tuition at NITech is ¥535,800 per year, and nondegree research students pay ¥356,400 per year.

[Apply to]

nit.nyushi@adm.nitech.ac.jp

[Links]   Web: **nitech.ac.jp** Twitter: **@nitechofficial**

- **Don't be afraid of failure.**
  Failure is an inevitable part of entrepreneurship and research. Whether or not you can take on challenges without fearing them will determine whether you will be able to grow.

- **Have a desire to change the world.**
  Whatever you do, we want it to benefit people and society.

- **Show the ability to work.**
  Bicycles fall when they are stationary and stand when they move. People and society can only move if people move. We want people who move.

- **Students should exhibit free and ethical thinking.**
  Free thinking and knowing your own beliefs are critical. Additionally, we believe that a person who has an ethical view of society will be successful.

- **Be aware of the world.**
  Common sense is always changing. Those who possess an awareness of the world and aspire to interact and change with it can have the most impact.

[Name] # Nagoya University

[Elevator Pitch] *"Nagoya University is a leading national university. It has nine faculties and thirteen graduate schools that span the humanities and sciences, and has produced six Nobel Prize winners from among its faculty members."*

[Enrollment] **Total enrollment: 16,000 (2019)**

[Description] Nagoya University started as a medical school in 1871 and has evolved into one of the country's leading educational institutions, offering both undergraduate and graduate courses as well as research opportunities. Six of the many Japanese laureates to receive the Nobel Prize in the twenty-first century were related with Nagoya University, and the university's educational and research programs are characterized by collaboration and interaction with institutions throughout Asia. The school has strong English-language programs that support its commitment to internationalization and attract talent from all over the world to Nagoya. Priding itself on a free and vibrant academic culture, the school has also committed to contribute to society and to pursue gender equality. It aims to cultivate talented people who can exercise strong leadership in a rapidly changing world.

In recent years, the university has increased its efforts to foster startups, providing incubation facilities, a support system for university-launched venture companies and several human resources exchange events, including the Tongali Project. The university's integrated support system also includes collaboration with venture funds, coordination with corporate partners, fundraising support and global business-development opportunities in partnership with foreign universities.

Nagoya University is particularly focused on startups in the manufacturing industry, a hallmark of the region. It offers opportunities for research, development and prototyping for deeptech innovations through collaborations among industry, academia and the private sector. The university has produced more than two hundred startups in the Tokai region and helped raise more than ¥30 billion in funding. In July 2020, Nagoya University was recognized as a Startup Ecosystem Global Center of Excellence by the Cabinet Office of Japan in recognition of its outstanding human resources, research and development capabilities, corporate activities and funding.

[Apply to] en.nagoya-u.ac.jp/contact_us/index.html

[Links]   Web: **en.nagoya-u.ac.jp** Facebook: **nagoya.university.en** Twitter: @NagoyaUniv

- **Know why you want an MBA.**
  You should understand the value of obtaining an MBA to prepare yourself for the challenges and growth it will require. A large part of this understanding should come from knowing where the degree will take you and what you will do with it once you are there.

- **Be a leader.**
  You should be able to document your leadership experiences and articulate the value of them.

- **Have ethics.**
  Students should know their own values and be able to capably defend their ideas of right and wrong to those with differing viewpoints.

- **Possess communication skills.**
  Learning through the case method and field method is accomplished through communication. We look for students who communicate well.

- **Understand how to think logically.**
  You should be proficient in employing deductive and inductive reasoning to make meaningful contributions to postgraduate-level class discussions.

[Name] # NUCB Business School

[Elevator Pitch] *"We emphasize learning through practical models, such as participant-centered learning in courses taught in the case method and field method. We have earned accreditation from two influential business school accreditation organizations: the AACSB International and the AMBA."*

[Enrollment] **Total enrollment: 900 (2018)**

[Description] The Nagoya University of Commerce and Business (NUCB) was founded in 1953 by Dr. Yuichi Kurimoto, the first Japanese student to graduate from the University of Alberta in Canada. It offers both undergraduate and graduate level programs, including the only English BBA in Japan. The NUCB Business School opened in 1990 and launched its MBA program in April 2000. In 2003, it inaugurated the first weekend MBA program in Japan. The school prides itself on producing "distinguished leaders who take the initiative in reforming established business activities and starting new ventures to contribute to society's advancement."

Most of the students at NUCB Business School are executives, and about 40 percent of all courses at the school are designated as Executive MBA courses. Enrollment in the Executive MBA program requires ten to fifteen years of professional experience, and MBA candidates account for approximately 80 percent of the student body. The NUCB Business School offers the only internationally accredited MBA program in the central Japan region and it is entirely different from programs at other Japanese business schools. Its purpose is not just to provide knowledge to graduates, but also to get them working. The school's alumni network is part of this process, organizing study groups in a variety of categories across specialized areas several times a year.

Budding entrepreneurs can receive support through the Incubation Center and Center for Entrepreneurs, which are both focused on prestartup assistance. They emphasize the generation and improvement of ideas at a very early stage through fieldwork, asking students to get out of the classroom and consult with as many people as possible. The school's philosophy starts from the standpoint that there is no one-size-fits-all method of doing business. Instead, it teaches the PDCA method (plan, do, check, act), an approach towards entrepreneurship that proposes taking time and effort to talk through ideas with others who have experience.

[Apply to] mba.nucba.ac.jp/en/admission/requirement.html

[Links] Web: **mba.nucba.ac.jp** Facebook: **NUCB.MBA** Twitter: **@mba_jp** Instagram: **mba_jp**

inve

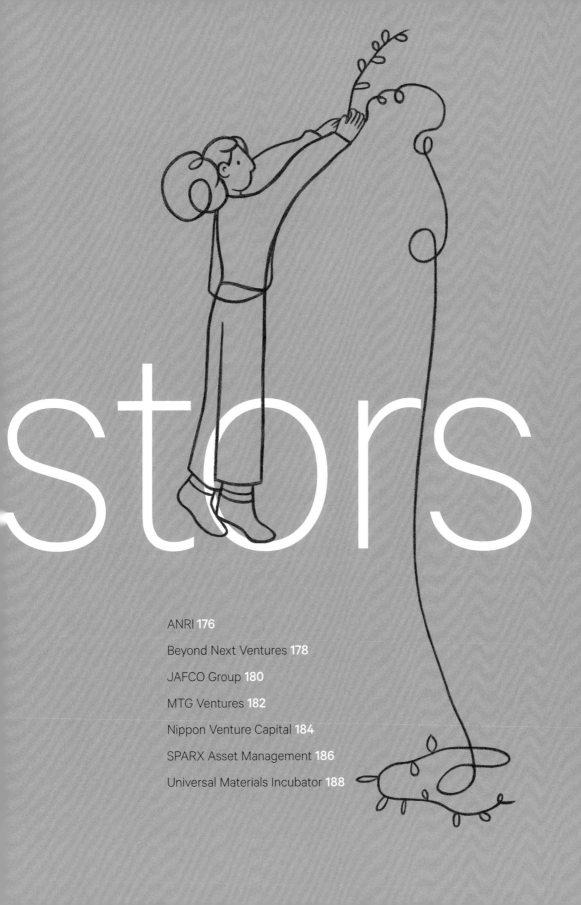

stors

- **Demonstrate grit.**
  When you launch a startup, you will face many
  challenges and difficult situations. Therefore,
  you need grit and persistence until you succeed.

- **Identify a real problem.**
  Find a problem in the market that needs solving.

- **Be obsessed with creating a solution.**
  You should be focused on changing the world
  or creating a product that solves world problems.

- **Demonstrate efficiency.**
  Particularly in the deeptech sector, your product
  needs to be ten times as successful than competing
  products.

- **Be cheaper.**
  Be as cheap as possible and more effective than
  the competition.

[Name]	# ANRI

[Elevator Pitch]

"We are one of the largest seed- and early-stage venture capital firms in Japan."

[Sector]

IT, SaaS, deeptech

[Description]

Founded in 2012 by Anri Samata, ANRI's first round of fundraising amassed $4 million. Since then, it has undertaken four further rounds of investment, and the firm currently has $300 million in assets under management. ANRI is involved in seed-stage investment at approximately $200,000–$300,000 but has also participated in Series A, B and C funding. In some instances, it will fund further investment rounds to as much as $20 million. Increasingly, its investments are in serial entrepreneurs with successful first companies.

When investing in the deeptech sector, ANRI looks for projects that will result in products that are ten times cheaper than the existing competition; otherwise, it deems them not profitable. According to ANRI partner Masahiro Sameshima, "Core competence is essential for deeptech or frontier tech startups to become viable." When asked about the Nagoya business environment, he says, "In the case of Nagoya, there is a higher concentration of businesses. There are many large companies concentrated in the same area, so we can take advantage of the location to develop new products and services. For example, an autonomous-driving concept car is already under development. Toyota has taken a step forward to finishing the project and bringing it to actual implementation."

One of ANRI's most successful investments to date is Raskul, a B2B platform that operates in the printing, logistics and advertising space. Raskul is part of the sharing economy and offers affordable pricing. It also invested in UUUM, one of the first agencies to manage YouTubers who are carving out profitable careers both in Japan and across the globe.

[Apply to]   info@anri.vc

[Links]   Web: **anri.vc** Twitter: **@NestHongo**

- **We are looking for businesses that can scale significantly.**
  Venture capital is a high-risk, high-reward business. If we're going to take that risk, we have to get a return on our investment.

- **Know your market size.**
  We are looking for business ideas that appeal to a large market.

- **Have a solid management team.**
  We look for startups with a president and a capable core management team that can help the company attract further investment.

- **Have the ability to execute a plan.**
  We look for managers who can make decisions and who have the ability to execute their plan and get results.

[Name]
Beyond Next Ventures

[Elevator Pitch]
"We established our venture capital company with the idea that Japanese universities have all sorts of potential seed companies with fantastic technological innovations but need funding and help with management know-how to develop into successful businesses."

[Sector]
Sector-agnostic

[Description]
Tsuyoshi Ito founded Beyond Next Ventures in 2014, after working for VC firm JAFCO for several years. Beyond Next Ventures launched its first fund in February 2015, ultimately raising ¥5.5 billion. The firm has a core mission to grow and harness the potential of motivated entrepreneurs with revolutionary technology, and commercialize their ideas to help build a better future and society. Around 60–70 percent of investments to date have been in the medical and life sciences fields, and it mainly invests in Japanese university-launched ventures during the seed phase.

In keeping with its aim to foster an environment that stimulates maximum productivity and growth for entrepreneurs, Beyond Next Ventures also provides professional assistance and resources to the companies it invests in, supporting the commercialization of their products and the development of new industries and talent. The firm has in-house headhunters and a matching platform to find appropriate candidates for projects needing leaders, and to connect researchers and businesspeople looking to commercialize. In 2016, it launched BRAVE, Japan's largest acceleration program for technical seed-stage ventures. It also operates the Blockbuster TOKYO acceleration program, which is hosted jointly with the Tokyo Metropolitan Government and is specialized in drug discovery. In addition, selected biotech startups can make use of a shared laboratory space provided by Beyond Next Ventures to help develop their products in an affordable way.

Beyond Next Ventures is currently managing a fund for Nagoya University and its investments include Nagoya-based Photo Electron Soul, which researches, develops and manufactures photocathode electron-beam systems. Since its second fund launched in October 2018, Beyond Next Ventures has also expanded its investments to foreign companies. Currently, it has five investments in India and is looking to invest about $20 million in Indian startups in the future.

[Apply to]
form.k3r.jp/beyondnextventures/200401

[Links]
Web: **beyondnextventures.com** LinkedIn: **company/beyond-next-ventures**
Facebook: **BeyondNextVentures** Twitter: **@BeyondNextV**

- **Have a clear management philosophy.**
  Don't just look at the market – have a philosophy about what you want to do.

- **What is your target market?**
  We are looking to invest in markets that are growing rapidly.

- **Be aware of timing.**
  We look at the startup's timing, the timing of the funding and the timing of market growth. These three factors should align.

- **Consider your return on investment.**
  Does your business have a return on investment relative to the size of our investment? We evaluate whether the business will be able to turn a profit.

- **It's all about personality.**
  At the end of the day, we decide whether to invest based on the personality of the founders. To work well together, not only do they need to be chosen by us, but we need to be chosen by them.

[Name]	# JAFCO Group

[Elevator Pitch] *"We are the most established venture capital firm in Japan. Our fund size is large, with over ¥400 billion under management. We invest in all types of industries and have also been active in Nagoya and the central Japan region for more than thirty years."*

[Sector] **Sector-agnostic**

[Description] JAFCO Group is an independent venture capital firm that has been active for over forty years. It was founded in Japan and has expanded into other parts of Asia and the US. Within each region, a local team identifies potential candidates, makes investments and provides post-investment support. Originally, funds were raised from partners with whom the company had an established relationship. In 2003, it changed its policy and began to seek funds more broadly to take advantage of an expanded venture market. It created a fund of ¥50 billion and established a revenue base through management fees. In addition to funds raised from external investors, 30–40 percent of total commitments are invested by JAFCO Group, meaning that fund performance is directly connected to JAFCO Group and its shareholders' profits.

JAFCO Group is open to investment in any industry but is actively seeking investments in AI, robotics, life sciences and digital transformation. Currently, 70–80 percent of the companies JAFCO Group invests in are early-stage and startups. Initial investment is usually ¥300 million to ¥500 million. The firm looks for companies in a fast-growing market or a market that is subject to rapid change. It values companies that have a highly principled management team and a strong sense of mission, as well as evidence of growth potential.

Two notable local investments JAFCO Group has made are in Tier IV, which originated at Nagoya University and is realizing autonomous driving by creating intelligent vehicles, and Nagoya-based stmn, a consulting service that utilizes cloud technology to foster better connections between companies and their employees.

[Apply to] ir@jafco.co.jp

[Links] Web: **jafco.co.jp** Facebook: **JAFCO.PR** Twitter: **@JAFCO_PR**

- **What kind of person are you?**
  Your drive and determination are more important
  to us than your business idea.

- **Be passionate about solving problems.**
  We are looking for a company led by an entrepreneur
  who seriously wants to make the world a better place.

- **Be prepared to compete globally.**
  Success in Japan is just part of it. You have to take
  a look at how you are going to compete globally from
  the beginning.

- **Aim to be the best in your field.**
  In a competitive market, you cannot survive unless
  you aspire to be number one.

- **Have a moonshot idea.**
  If you don't have an extremely ambitious project, your
  future will be smaller. Destructive and creative ideas
  can overwhelm the world and have a great impact
  on society. To change the world requires a great
  aspiration and perspective.

[Name]
MTG Ventures

[Elevator Pitch] *"We are a corporate venture capital firm investing in beauty-, wellness-, food- and sports- technology startups. We are unique because our parent company develops and markets such products and applies its strength to portfolio companies."*

[Sector] **Tech related to beauty, food, sports and wellness**

[Description] Established in 2018, MTG Ventures is a wholly owned subsidiary of MTG, a company that both brands and sells products related to beauty, wellness, food and sports. As a corporate venture capital fund (CVC), its investment is much smaller than that of other VCs, at about ¥100 million. MTG Ventures is primarily looking to invest at the seed stage and is open to startups outside of Japan. "We want to expand to China, Taiwan and India," says CEO Go Fujita. "Also, because we are a beauty and wellness investment company, we would like to have a female perspective as well as a male one. In the future, I would like to have some female members. They don't have to be Japanese. I want to expand the beauty and wellness business in Asia."

Having MTG behind it means that MTG Ventures can leverage its parent company's branding, marketing and sales strengths to promote the companies it invests in and realize profitable returns. The investor is looking for both synergies and capital gains. "We'll do it!" says Go. "The biggest difference between a CVC and a VC is whether you seek business synergies."

While MTG Ventures primarily supports early-stage companies, it also plays a role as a mentor to other startups in the central Japan region. It seeks out companies that are passionate about solving challenging problems, that have entrepreneurial spirit and that can compete globally. In Nagoya, it has invested in Tier IV, which is working on autonomous driving technology, and stmn, which has developed a cloud-based platform focused on employee retention and job satisfaction.

[Apply to] info.mtgv@mtg.gr.jp

[Links] Web: mtg.gr.jp/company/group/mtg-ventures Facebook: MTGVentures Twitter: @MTGVentures

- **Bring in good people.**
  You can't grow a company on your own,
  so the ability to involve the best people is vital
  to building a successful business.

- **Be able to create a story.**
  How are you going to get where you are going? You
  need to be able to explain it so we can invest in you.

- **Know what you are going to do with the funding.**
  Just owning a few billion in stocks is not enough
  to take you to where you need to go.

- **Provide something that society is looking for.**
  Are you offering something that society needs
  or wants? Can you provide it? We are looking
  to invest in a business that has a market.

[Name] # Nippon Venture Capital

[Elevator Pitch] *"We are one of the largest independent venture capital firms in Japan, providing a full range of services and infrastructure to entrepreneurial companies seeking to contribute to the Japanese economy while simultaneously advancing their earnings."*

[Sector] **Sector-agnostic**

[Description] Established in 1996, Nippon Venture Capital has invested in over a thousand companies to date. Of these, 148 are listed companies. The firm is open to investments in any industry, but has a focus on seed- and early-stage Japanese companies. Ventures are supported on a case-by-case basis, depending on their needs. When deciding whether to fund a startup, the firm looks for committed managers who work diligently with stakeholders and considers the venture's future potential. Social needs, competitiveness, evidence, quality and the management team's experience are also taken into account.

In addition, the firm has funds based on long associations with universities, including the Kyoto University Venture Fund and the Osaka Bio Fund. Nippon Venture Capital also maintains a joint venture fund with five regional universities in the Tokai region, including Nagoya University, which invests in research ventures. The firm goes further than providing financial support. It also works with the universities it funds to provide entrepreneurial advice to aspiring founders and offers support even in the initial stages before they start a business.

Nippon Venture Capital has funded Ficha, which develops image-recognition software that is mainly used in in-vehicle cameras and drive recorders to detect pedestrians, vehicles and road signs. It has also funded PREVENT, which created an algorithm that can project target patients with a high probability of a serious medical event, and APTJ, which develops software platforms for vehicle-control systems. Most of Nippon Venture Capital's investments come by referral, but it is also open to applications through its website.

[Apply to] nvcc.co.jp/en/contact-us

[Links] Web: **nvcc.co.jp**

- **Present a vision and a strategy to implement it.**
  First and foremost is the management team's clear vision and strategy.

- **Have a quality management team.**
  The most crucial factor is your management team and whether it has a strong will and high aspirations to solve social issues.

- **Have a market.**
  No matter how good the idea is, if there is no market to support it, it will not work as a business.

- **Have unique technology.**
  Does your company have the technology and business model to create a market? When you enter a market, your business model needs to incorporate unique technology.

SPARX Asset Management

[Name]

[Elevator Pitch] *"In business for over three decades, we invest in globally listed companies, unlisted companies and real assets such as real estate and renewable power plants."*

[Sector] **AI, robotics, solar and hydrogen technology**

[Description] SPARX Asset Management (SPARX) was one of the first companies to adopt investment strategies new to Japan through its investments in listed companies. Unlike other institutional investors, SPARX's founders decided not to look for customers in-country. They determined that the firm couldn't compete with the big players and thus needed a unique strategy. Instead, it would play the role of a pilot for foreign investors in Japan. It began by specializing in long/short equity strategies focused on small- and mid-cap investments, which helped it become a significant player.

The firm began to actively invest in the solar technology sector, creating a solar power fund in 2013 under the assumption that the era of renewable energy was at hand. SPARX raised over ¥200 billion to invest in solar power plants. In 2015, it launched venture capital fund Mirai Creation Fund with investments from Toyota, Sumitomo Mitsui Banking and others to target the areas of intelligent technologies (including AI), robotics, hydrogen technology, electrification and new materials. The Mirai Creation Fund has a track record of investing in promising companies around the world. Its goal is to contribute to the society of the future by investing in companies that are world leaders in innovative technologies and business models.

SPARX participates in all stages of funding from seed to Series A, B and C, at times going beyond these stages and undertaking further financing. The firm has invested in Nagoya-based Meijo NanoCarbon, which supplies high-purity single-walled carbon nanotubes, and Tier IV, which creates self-driving platforms, among other Japanese startups.

[Apply to] sparx.co.jp/contact.php

[Links] Web: sparx.co.jp Facebook: SPARXGroup

- **Have solid technology.**
  We are looking for reliable technology that is globally competitive.

- **Focus on customer satisfaction.**
  Is your customer happy? No matter how great your technology's performance, it doesn't matter if the customer isn't pleased. The benefit to the customer must be clear.

- **Create the right management team.**
  We believe that half of the success of our investment projects is due to people. Of course, the technology and business model must be solid, but the management team is essential.

- **Be enthusiastic and informed.**
  First and foremost is enthusiasm – you must have the zeal to do whatever it takes to make your company a success. On top of that, you should complement your management team and have a solid understanding of your technology and business model.

[Name]
Universal Materials Incubator

[Elevator Pitch] *"We are a venture capital firm that aims to be a new business-creation platform specializing in the materials science field."*

[Sector] **Materials science**

[Description] Universal Materials Incubator (UMI) is a venture capital firm specializing in chemicals and materials science. Through providing both financial investment and business development support, it aims to help create new businesses in the materials and chemical industry, a sector comparable in size to the automobile industry. UMI's first fund, established in January 2016, raised ¥10 billion. Its parent company, INCJ, and nine other materials and chemical companies invested. A second fund was established in April 2019, which raised ¥9.5 billion. Fifteen materials and chemical companies and four financial institutions have invested in this second fund.

UMI's focus is on scaling up, but it also invests in promising seed-stage startups and in new business projects in large companies. The amount of funding provided is determined on a case-by-case basis. It can be difficult to envision sustainable business models for new materials, and commercialization is traditionally a lengthy process, so UMI nurtures collaboration with global corporate partners and maintains strong ties to universities with an aim of making the development, production and application of new materials more efficient and profitable.

The firm is the only VC in Japan that specializes in materials science, and one of very few such firms globally. UMI was founded with a vision of strengthening Japan's technological capabilities by fostering outstanding materials and chemical companies, and cultivating an industry structure that can compete in the global arena. To achieve this, it uses its international network to find new startups and promising technologies, and encourages referrals from materials science companies and other VCs. Its connections to academia and research allow it to keep abreast of innovations including new methods of reducing CO_2, water treatment and food and agriculture technologies.

[Apply to] **umi.co.jp/en/contact**

[Links] Web: **umi.co.jp/en** LinkedIn: **company/universal-materials-incubator-co.-ltd.**

directory

The following selection is a brief choice of organizations, companies and contacts available in **Nagoya**

Startups

Craif
Furocho
Nagoya-shi
Chikusa-ku
464-0814
craif.com

GRA&GREEN
Room 106, Incubation Facility
Nagoya University
1 Furocho
Chikusa-ku
Nagoya 464-0814
gragreen.com

iBody
102 Incubation Facility
Nagoya University
1 Furocho
Chikusa-ku
Nagoya 464-0814
ibody.co.jp

i Smart Technologies
7-26 Nakayamamachi
Hekinan 447-0035
istc.co.jp

Optimind
9F, Central Building
11-30-2 Sakae
Naka-ku
Nagoya 460-0008
optimind.tech

Prodrone
1-115 Nakahira
Tenpaku-ku
Nagoya 468-0014
prodrone.com

stmn
1-1 Ibuka-cho
Nakamura-ku
Nagoya 453-0012
stmn.co.jp

Tier IV
Jacom Building
1-12-10 Kitashinagawa
Shinagawa-ku
Tokyo 140-0001
tier4.jp

TOWING
7-1 Maehamatori
Minami-ku
Nagoya 457-0058
towing.co.jp

TRYETING
Central Nagoya Aoi 4F
1-20-22 Aoi
Naka-ku
Nagoya 460-0006
tryeting.jp

United Immunity
Room 220, Mie University
Campus Incubator
1577 Kurimamachiya-cho
Tsu, Mie 514-8507
unitedimmunity.co.jp

Programs

Beyond the Border
Nagoya Innovator's Garage
Nadya Park 4F
3-18-1 Sakae
Naka-ku
Nagoya 460-0008
garage-nagoya.or.jp/
program/p3144

NAGOYA BOOST 10000
Startup Support Office
Innovation Promotion
Department
Nagoya City Economic
Affairs Bureau
3-1-1 Sannomaru Naka-ku
Nagoya 460-8508
nagoyaboost.jp

Nagoya ICT Innovation Lab
Next-Generation Industry
Promotion Division
Innovation Promotion
Department
Nagoya City Economic
Affairs Bureau
3-1-1 Sannomaru Naka-ku
Nagoya 460-8508
nagoya-innovation.jp/
nagoya-mirai/ict

Tongali Project
Nagoya University National
Innovation Complex
Furocho
Chikusa-ku
Nagoya 464-8601
tongali.net

Spaces

**Meijo University Social
Collaboration Zone Shake**
4-102-9 Yadaminami
Higashi-ku
Nagoya 461-8534
plat.meijo-u.ac.jp/shake

Midland Incubators House
Room 142, Shin Nagoya
Center Building
Honjin-gai
1-1 Ibukacho
Nakamura-ku
Nagoya 453-0012
m15s.jp

**MUSASHi Innovation Lab
CLUE**
Cocola Avenue 3F
1 Chome-135 Ekimae Odori
Toyohashi
Aichi 440-0888
musashi.co.jp/clue

Nagono Campus
2-14-1 Nagono
Nishi-ku
Nagoya 451-0042
nagono-campus.jp

Nagoya Innovator's Garage
Nadya Park 4F
3-18-1 Sakae
Naka-ku
Nagoya 460-0008
garage-nagoya.or.jp

WeWork Global Gate Nagoya
4-60-12 Hiraikecho
Nakamura-ku
Nagoya 453-6111
wework.com/buildings/
global-gate-nagoya--nagoya

Some of the websites in the Directory require the 'www' prefix.

Experts

IBIDEN
2-1 Kanda-cho
Ogaki
Gifu 503-8604
ibiden.com

Nippon Telegraph and Telephone West
4-9-60 Osu 4-Chome
Naka-ku
Nagoya 460-8319
ntt-west.co.jp

PwC Japan Group
Global Innovation Factory
PwC Consulting LLC
2-6-1 Marunouchi
Chiyoda-ku
Tokyo 100-6921
pwc.com/jp/en

Toyota Industries
2-1 Toyoda-cho
Kariya-shi
Aichi 448-8671
toyota-industries.com

Founders

ABEJA
WeWork the ARGYLE Aoyama
2-14-4 Kitaaoyama
Minato-ku
Tokyo 107-0061
abejainc.com

CURUCURU
Onaga Building 7F
1-11-20 Nishiki
Naka-ku
Nagoya 460-0003
curucuru.co.jp

M2 Labo
1076-2 Nunohikihara
Makinohara
Shizuoka 421-0407
m2-labo.jp

SPEED
North Side, 3rd Floor, Tsubasa Building
4-14-18 Osu
Naka-ku
Nagoya 460-0011
speedinc-jp.com

Miraiproject
Izumi First Square 8F
1-21-27, Izumi 1
Higashi-ku
Nagoya 461-0001
miraiproject.co.jp

Schools

Aichi University of the Arts
1-114 Sagamine
Yazako
Nagakute-shi
Aichi 480-1194
aichi-fam-u.ac.jp

GLOBIS University
JR Gate Tower 27F
1-1-3 Meieki
Nakamura-ku
Nagoya 450-6627
mba.globis.ac.jp

Kinjo Gakuin University
2-1723 Omori
Moriyama-ku
Nagoya Aichi 463-8521
kinjo-u.ac.jp

Nagoya Institute of Technology
Gokiso-cho
Showa-ku
Nagoya 466-8555
nitech.ac.jp

Nagoya University
Furocho
Chikusa-ku
Nagoya 464-8601
en.nagoya-u.ac.jp

NUCB Business School
1-3-1 Nishiki
Naka-ku
Nagoya 460-0003
mba.nucba.ac.jp

Investors

ANRI
2 Chome-6-6
Shibuya
Shibuya City
Tokyo 150-0002
anri.vc

Beyond Next Ventures
MFPR Nihonbashi Honcho Building 3F
3-7-2 Nihonbashi-honcho
Chuo-ku
Tokyo 103-0023
beyondnextventures.com

JAFCO Group
FLEZIO LA 8F
3-19-5 Marunouchi
Naka-ku
Nagoya 460-0002
jafco.co.jp

MTG Ventures
Office Omori 8F
2-8-24 Nishiki
Naka-ku
Nagoya 460-0003
mtg.gr.jp/company/group/mtg-ventures

Nippon Venture Capital
2-4-1 Marunouchi
Chiyoda-ku
Tokyo 100-6334
nvcc.co.jp

SPARX Asset Management
Shinagawa Season Terrace 6F
1-2-70 Konan
Minato-ku
Tokyo 108-0075
sparx.co.jp

Universal Materials Incubator
Konwa Building 4F
Tsukiji 1-12-22
Chuo-ku
Tokyo 104-0045
umi.co.jp/en

Accommodation

Aichi Prefectural Housing Corporation
aichi-kousha.or.jp

Hilton Hotels and Resorts
hiltonhotels.jp/hotel/chubu/
hilton-nagoya

Interlink
interlinkjapan.com

Japan Home Search
japanhomesearch.com

Japan Mobility
japan-mobility.com

Marriott Nagoya Associa
associa.com/nma/
multi-lingual

Nagoya Kanko Hotel
nagoyakankohotel.co.jp/en

Nagoya Tokyu Hotel
tokyuhotelsjapan.com/
global/nagoya-h

Nissho
nissho-apn.co.jp/chintai/
houjin/index_en.html

Sumaino Ichiban
english.sumaino1ban.jp

Tomei Homes
tomeihomes.co.jp

Banks

Aichi Bank
aichibank.co.jp

Japan Post Holdings
japanpost.jp/en

MUFG
bk.mufg.jp/global

Mizuho
mizuhogroup.com/bank

SMBC
smbc.co.jp/global

The Bank of Nagoya
meigin.com/index.html

The Chukyo Bank
chukyo-bank.co.jp

Coffee Shops and Places with Wifi

Komeda's Coffee
3-20-13 Nishiki
Naka-ku
Nagoya 460-0003
komeda.co.jp/index_en.php

Maison YWE
3-23-9 Sakae
Naka-ku
Nagoya 460-0008
maison-ywe.jp

Mitts Coffee Stand
2-8-15 Nishiki
Naka-ku
Nagoya 460-0003
facebook.com/
MittsCoffeeStand

Nagonoya
1-6-13 Nagono
Nishi-ku
Nagoya 451-0042
nagonoya.com/cms/
english.html

Royal Garden Cafe Nagoya
Richmond Hotel Nagoya
Nayabashi 1F
1-2-7 Sakae
Naka-ku
Nagoya 460-0008
royal-gardencafe.com/nagoya

The Cups
2-14-1 Nishiki
Naka-ku
Nagoya 460-0003
cups.co.jp/location.html

YABA Coffee shop
4-1-21 Osu
Naka-ku
Nagoya 460-0011
central-hld.jp/yaba-coffee

Groups and Meetups

The American Chamber of Commerce in Japan Chūbu Chapter
Marunouchi Fukao Buillding 5F
2-11-24 Marunouchi
Naka-ku
Nagoya 460-0002
accj.or.jp/chubu-chapter-1

Aichi International Association
Aichi Prefectural Government
Sannomaru Annex 1&2F
2-6-1 Sannomaru
Naka-ku
Nagoya 460-0001
aia.pref.aichi.jp/tope/
index.html

Nagoya Connect
venturecafetokyo.org/
nagoya-connect

Nagoya Expat Help
facebook.com/
groups/750194835043203

Tokai Japan Canada Society
tjcs.jp

Useful Resources

Central Japan Economic Federation
Nagoya Sakae Building 10F
5-1 Buhei-cho
Higashi-ku
Nagoya 461-0008
chukeiren.or.jp/en

Greater Nagoya Initiative
Ikko Osu Building 7F
1-35-18 Osu
Naka-ku
Nagoya 460-0011
greaternagoya.org/en

I-BAC
Nagoya Chamber of
Commerce & Industry
Building 7F
2-10-19 Sakae
Naka-ku
Nagoya 460-0008
i-bac.jp

Japan 24-Hour Helpline
japanhelpline.com/about-us

JETRO
Aichi Industry & Labor
Center 18F
4-4-38 Meieki
Nakamura-ku
Nagoya 450-0002
jetro.go.jp/en

Nagoya International Center
Nagoya International Center
Building 3F
1-47-1 Nagono
Nakamura-ku
Nagoya 450-0001
nic-nagoya.or.jp/en

Financial Services

Deloitte Tohmatsu Financial Advisory LLC
deloitte.com/jp/en

EY Japan
ey.com/en_jp

KPMG
home.kpmg/jp/en

PwC Japan Group
pwc.com/jp/en

Smart Tax Nagoya
40 Inoue-cho
Chikusa-ku
Nagoya 464-0026
smartaxnagoya.wordpress.com

Yuji Suzuki USA Tax Office
usa-zeiri.com

Important Government Offices

Aichi Industry and Labor Center
4-4-38 Meieki
Nakamura-ku
Nagoya 450-0002
winc-aichi.jp/en

Aichi Prefectural Government
3-1-2 Sannomaru
Naka-ku
Nagoya 460-8501
pref.aichi.jp/global/en/
index.html

Nagoya City
3-1-1 Sannomaru
Naka-ku
Nagoya 460-8508
city.nagoya.jp/en/index.html

Insurance Companies

Aioi Nissay Dowa Insurance
aioinissaydowa.co.jp/english

AXA General Insurance
axa-direct.co.jp

Hoken no Madoguchi
hokennomadoguchi.com

Manulife Life Insurance
manulife.co.jp/ja/
individual.html

Mitsui Sumitomo Insurance
ms-ins.com/english

SOMPO JAPAN Insurance
sompo-japan.co.jp/english

Tokio Marine & Nichido Fire Insurance
tokiomarine-nichido.co.jp/en

VIVAVIDA!
vivavida.net/en

Zurich Insurance
zurich.co.jp

Language Schools

ECC Japanese Language Institute
Kanayama Building 5F
1-16-16 Kanayama
Naka-ku
Nagoya 460-0022
ecc-nihongo.com/en/nagoya

I.C. Nagoya
Meieki-Nagata Building
3-26-19 Meieki
Nakamura-ku
Nagoya 450-0002
icn.gr.jp

**JSLN Japanese
Language School**
Utoku Building 8F
1-28-26 Meiekiminami
Nakamura-ku
Nagoya 450-0003
jslnagoya.com/en

**Nagoya YWCA School
of Japanese Language**
2-3 Shinsakaemachi
Naka-ku
Nagoya 460-0004
ywca.nagoya/en

WARAKU Japan
Meikou Building 2F
1-17-13 Nishiki
Naka-ku
Nagoya 460-0003
waraku-japan.com

Legal Services

**Jackson Sogo
Gyoseishoshi Law Office**
jacksonsogo.com

**Nagoya International
Law Office**
nagoya-intlaw.com/en

Nagoya Legal Office
nagoyalegal.com

Office GLocals
Room 303
3-13 Kikusaka
Chikusa-ku
Nagoya 464-0836
en.office-glocals.com

Relo Japan
relojapan.com/our-services/
immigration

Yuji Suzuki USA Tax Office
usa-zeiri.com

Startup Events

**Central Japan Open
Innovation Pitch**
garage-nagoya.or.jp

Nagoya Boost Day
nagoyaboost.jp

Nagoya Connect
venturecafetokyo.org/
nagoya-connect

**One Japan Hackathon
x Tokai**
onejapan-hackathon-tokai.jp

Startup Weekend Nagoya
swnagoya.doorkeeper.jp

**Tongali Business Plan
Contest**
tongali.net/tag/t-bizcon

Nagoya City Science Museum – Nagoya, Japan

glossary

A

AaaS (algorithm as a service) — an algorithm based on the cloud so users can develop, run and use algorithms on a platform without incurring the cost and effort of buying and maintaining the underlying architecture

accelerator — an organization or program that offers advice and resources to help small businesses grow

AI (artificial intelligence) — the simulation of human intelligence by computer systems; machines that are able to perform tasks normally carried out by humans

angel investment — outside funding with shared ownership equity typically made possible by an affluent individual who provides a startup with starting capital

[see also: **business angel**]

B

backcasting — a planning method that starts with defining a desired outcome and then works backwards to identify actions that will make that outcome possible

B2B (business-to-business) — the exchange of services, information and/or products from a business to a business

B2C (business-to-consumer) — the exchange of services, information and/or products from a business to a consumer

bootstrapping — to self-fund, without outside investment

business angel — an experienced entrepreneur or professional who provides starting capital for promising startups

[see also: **angel investment**]

C

C-level — a corporate title given to high-ranking executives responsible for making company-wide decisions

CEO (chief executive officer) — the highest-ranking person in a company, responsible for taking on managerial decisions

COO (chief operating officer) — a high-level executive running the operations of a company

coworking space — a shared working environment

D

deep learning — a subfield of machine learning concerned with algorithms inspired by the structure and function of neural networks

deeptech — technology focused on autonomous systems, including robotics and smart devices

E

early-stage — the stage in which financing is provided by a venture capital firm to a company after the seed round; a company stage in which a product or service is still in development but not on the market yet

edge computing — computing at the source of data to decrease latency

elevator pitch — a short description of an idea, product or company that explains the concept

F

fintech — financial technology; a technology or innovation that aims to compete with traditional financial methods in the delivery of financial services

flex desk — a shared desk available for temporary use in a coworking space

fog computing — computing, storage and networking services between end devices and cloud computing

G

Galapagosization — the application of Galápagos syndrome, a term used to refer to an isolated development branch of a globally available product

H

HACCP (hazard analysis and critical control points) — a system that offers a preventative approach to food safety

I

ICT (internet and communications technology) — technology, such as computers, the internet and telecommunications, that is used to create, store and exchange information

incubator — a facility established to nurture young startup firms during their first few months or years of development

IoT (internet of things) — a network of objects utilizing sensors and software to exchange data over the internet

IPO (initial public offering) — the first time a company's stock is offered for sale to the public

K

kaizen — a Japanese business philosophy that focuses on continuous improvement and efficiency in personnel, processes and logistics

L

later-stage — the stage in which companies have typically demonstrated viability as a going concern and have a product with a strong market presence

M

monoclonal antibodies — antibodies that bind to almost any substance and are often used in "magic bullet" therapies to selectively deliver toxins to a disease-causing organism

monozukuri — "production" or "manufacturing." Also used to mean technological prowess, know-how and the spirit of Japan's manufacturing practices.

MVP (minimum viable product) — a product with just enough features to satisfy early customers who can provide feedback for future product development

P

pitch — an opportunity to introduce a business idea in a limited amount of time to potential investors, often using a presentation

R

R&D (research and development) — the process by which a company obtains new knowledge that it might use to create new technology, products or services

S

SaaS (software as a service) — a software distribution model in which a third-party provider hosts applications and makes them available to customers

seed funding — the first round of venture capital funding (typically called the seed round); a small, early-stage investment from family members, friends, banks or an investor, also known as a seed investor

Series A/B/C/D/E — the subsequent funding rounds that come after the seed stage and aim to raise further capital (up to $1 million) when the company demonstrates various increase factors

startup — companies under three years old that are in the growth stage and starting to become profitable (if not already)

U

use case — a list of actions or event steps defining the interactions between a role and a system to achieve a goal

V

VC (venture capital) — a form of financing that comes from a pool of investors in a venture capital firm in return for equity

STARTUP GUIDE JOHANNESBURG — The Entrepreneur's Handbook
STARTUP GUIDE HAMBURG — The Entrepreneur's Handbook
STARTUP GUIDE AMSTERDAM — The Entrepreneur's Handbook
STARTUP GUIDE CAPE TOWN — The Entrepreneur's Handbook
STARTUP GUIDE LUXEMBOURG — The Entrepreneur's Handbook
STARTUP GUIDE VIENNA — The Entrepreneur's Handbook
STARTUP GUIDE TEL AVIV — The Entrepreneur's Handbook
STARTUP GUIDE MADRID — The Entrepreneur's Handbook
STARTUP GUIDE COPENHAGEN — The Entrepreneur's Handbook
IMPACT GUIDE SERIES STARTUP GUIDE JAPAN — The Entrepreneur's Handbook
STARTUP GUIDE PARIS — The Entrepreneur's Handbook
STARTUP GUIDE LOS ANGELES — The Entrepreneur's Handbook
STARTUP GUIDE REYKJAVIK — The Entrepreneur's Handbook
STARTUP GUIDE STOCKHOLM — The Entrepreneur's Handbook
STARTUP GUIDE MUNICH — The Entrepreneur's Handbook
STARTUP GUIDE FRANKFURT — The Entrepreneur's Handbook
STARTUP GUIDE ZURICH — The Entrepreneur's Handbook
STARTUP GUIDE LONDON — The Entrepreneur's Handbook
STARTUP GUIDE TOKYO — The Entrepreneur's Handbook
STARTUP GUIDE LISBON — The Entrepreneur's Handbook
IMPACT GUIDE SERIES STARTUP GUIDE SWITZERLAND — The Entrepreneur's Handbook
STARTUP GUIDE SINGAPORE — The Entrepreneur's Handbook
STARTUP GUIDE NEW YORK — The Entrepreneur's Handbook
STARTUP GUIDE CAIRO — The Entrepreneur's Handbook
STARTUP GUIDE BANGKOK — The Entrepreneur's Handbook
STARTUP GUIDE BERLIN — The Entrepreneur's Handbook
IMPACT GUIDE SERIES STARTUP GUIDE LAGOS — The Entrepreneur's Handbook
IMPACT GUIDE SERIES STARTUP GUIDE ACCRA — The Entrepreneur's Handbook
IMPACT GUIDE SERIES STARTUP GUIDE NAIROBI — The Entrepreneur's Handbook
IMPACT GUIDE SERIES STARTUP GUIDE KIGALI — The Entrepreneur's Handbook

startupguide.com   Follow us: @StartupGuideHQ

About the Guide

Based on traditional guidebooks and stocked with information you might need to know about starting your next business adventure, Startup Guide books help you navigate and connect with different startup scenes across the globe. Each book is packed with exciting stories of entrepreneurship, insightful interviews with local experts and useful tips and tricks. To date, Startup Guide has featured over forty cities and regions in Europe, Asia, the US, Africa and the Middle East, including Berlin, London, Singapore, New York, Cape Town and Tel Aviv.

How we make the books:

To ensure an accurate and trustworthy guide every time, we team up with local partners that are established in their respective startup scene. We then ask the local community to nominate startups, coworking spaces, founders, schools, investors, incubators and established businesses to be featured through an online submission form. Based on the results, these submissions are narrowed down to the top one hundred organizations and individuals. Next, the local advisory board – which is selected by our community partners and consists of key players in the local startup community – votes for the final selection, ensuring a balanced representation of industries and startup stories in each book.
The local community partners then work in close collaboration with our international editorial and design team to help research, organize interviews with journalists and plan photoshoots. Finally, all content is reviewed and edited and the book is designed and created by the Startup Guide team before going to print in Berlin.

Where to find us:

The easiest way to get your hands on a Startup Guide book is to order it from our online shop: startupguide.com/shop. You can also visit us at our Lisbon and Copenhagen offices:

Rua Saraiva de Carvalho 1C
1250-240 Lisbon, Portugal
lisbon@startupguide.com

Borgbjergsvej 1,
2450 Copenhagen, Denmark
copenhagen@startupguide.com

Want to become a stockist or suggest a store?

Get in touch here: sales@gestalten.com

The Startup Guide Website

Since the first Startup Guide book was published, our network has grown and the possibilities to reach new audiences have expanded. One of the reasons we decided to start producing content through a digital platform was to be able to take a deeper look at the cities, regions and ecosystems that our books cover. We want to make it more accessible for new entrepreneurs to understand the process of getting a startup off the ground through the stories of those who were once in their shoes. By sharing educational content and inspiring examples from the startup community, our website provides valuable insights and continues our core purpose: to guide, empower and inspire people beginning their entrepreneurial path.

For more details, visit our website at startupguide.com.

#startupeverywhere

Startup Guide was founded by Sissel Hansen in 2014. As a publishing and media company, we produce guidebooks and online content to help entrepreneurs navigate and connect with different startup scenes across the globe. As the world of work changes, our mission stays the same: to guide, empower and inspire people to start their own business anywhere. To get your hands on one of our books, feel free to visit us at our offices in Lisbon and Copenhagen.

Want to learn more,
become a partner or just say hello?

Send us an email at info@startupguide.com

Follow us: @StartupGuideHQ
Join us and #startupeverywhere

Nagoya Advisory Board

Go Fujita
CEO
MTG Ventures

Goro Kamino
Director
Nippon Venture Capital

Hirooki Fujiwara
Director General
Nagoya Innovator's
Garage and Designated
Professor Strategic
Innovation Office,
Nagoya University

Kumiko Hidaka
Vice President,
Public Affairs
WeWork Japan

Michel Weenick
Vice President
Architecture and
Construction, Asia
Hilton Grand Vacations

Takahiro Makino
Founder
Miraiproject

Takami Yasuda
Professor
Nagoya University

Takashi Sasano
General Manager
Economic Research
Division
Central Japan Economic
Federation

Toshio Sumi
Director
Startup Support Office
Nagoya City

With thanks to our **Content Partners**

株式会社 豊田自動織機
TOYOTA INDUSTRIES CORPORATION

WHERE NEXT?